NAVIGATING CHAOS

How to Find Certainty in Uncertain Situations

NAVIGATING CHAOS

Former Navy SEAL and Executive Coach for Leadership,
Culture Change, and High Performance Teams

JEFF BOSS

To my Fallen Brothers. You will never be forgotten.

Michael Murphy

Clark Schwedler

Mark Carter

Tommy Valentine

Mike Koch

Nate Hardy

Lance Vaccaro

Sean Flynn

Josh Harris

Jason Friewald

John Marcum

Colin Thomas

Adam Brown

Extortion 17

Turbine 33

Brett Shadle

Nicolas Checque

*A portion of the proceeds from this book will be donated to the SEAL Future Fund. Visit www.sealfuturefund.org for more information.

A GENUINE ARCHER BOOK

ARCHER/RARE BIRD

601 West 26th Street · Suite 325 · New York · NY 10001
archerlit.com

FIRST HARDCOVER EDITION

Printed in the United States
Set in Minion

Publisher's Cataloging-in-Publication data

Names: Boss, Jeff, author.
Title: Navigating chaos : how to find certainty in uncertain situations / by Jeff Boss.
Description: First hardcover edition. | New York [New York] ; Los Angeles [California] : Archer,
2015 | Includes bibliographical references.
Identifiers: ISBN 978-1-941729-06-9
Subjects: LCSH: Leadership. | Self-actualization. | United States. Navy.
SEALs—Anecdotes. |
Executive coaching. | BISAC: Business & Economics | Leadership.
Classification: LCC HD57.7 B678 2015 | DDC 658.4—dc23

Contents

Introduction

This is not a book on how to be a badass, jump out of planes, or shoot a piece of barbed wire from a mile away—you know, the stuff that SEALs are famous for? Instead, what this book is about is how to *learn* to be a badass on your own—at whatever it is that you set your mind to achieving. As a teenager and an early adult, my life's mission was to become a Navy SEAL. That's what I worked toward and what I succeeded in. The principles that governed my learning process, however, are something that can be applicable to anyone who seeks to become a top-tier performer in whatever their chosen field happens to be. The professional football player or Fortune 500 CEO, yes, but also the stay-at-home mom or the twenty-five-year-old entrepreneur. Anyone who is seeking high performance has come to the right place.

Why the title *Navigating Chaos*? Because, as you will learn in this book, the ability to comport yourself in uncertain situations—which is actually most situations, if you really think about it—is the most important skill you need to develop if you are going to become a top-tier performer. I had the opportunity to learn this the hard way through thirteen years on the SEAL Teams, working at the highest level with other high-performing and hard-driving individuals. However, what you will learn about us from this book is that we are far from the one-dimensional, knuckle-dragging image that the public believes us to be.

Hollywood likes to portray SEALs with a shoot 'em up, almost larger-than-life persona that capitalizes on brawn and bravado, and unfortunately, that's the only image of us that much of the public will ever know. What is not shown, however, are the mental capacities and emotional tolerances that we strive to enhance on a daily basis through an organizational model of continuous improvement, shared understanding, humility, and leadership.

I never thought that I would want to write about anything even remotely related to special operations, let alone about something so "hush-hush" as the SEAL Teams. But there are lessons from the thirteen years I spent as a SEAL that should be shared.

It has been an internal struggle to write. The catch-22 of breaking the unspoken rule of not writing is to either do something that's enjoyable and fulfilling, or to remain forever in the shadows and forget the experiences that have made me who I am today; lessons that can be shared with others so *they* may improve.

If the intent behind writing this book were to be another SEAL-turned-author and to beat my chest out of arrogance, then I wouldn't have sent it to my publisher. That's not me, nor is that my purpose. My purpose in writing this book is to share knowledge with those who seek to address unanswered questions within and about themselves, their teams, and their companies; with executives who may benefit from an alternative perspective to help cope with seemingly unanswerable leadership demands; and with those who believe in constant and never-ending improvement. That's what this book is about. For the operational vignettes, I apologize to my brothers. However, just as any writer pulls from the context he or she knows best, I am pulling from mine—my experience just happens to fall within a realm that is frowned upon when shared. Deal with it.

The Teams are what have shaped me into the person I am today, and my naval career pathway brought with it knowledge and experience gained from unique situations that cannot be replicated in corporate America. Teamwork, superior performance, and the ability to overcome complex situations with limited resources can only be learned under the most austere conditions, such as those to which SEALs are exposed continually throughout our training and professional careers. These experiences shape our character, competence, life passion, family values, and humility in a way that nothing else ever could.

Be forewarned, however, that this is not a how-to book. I am not going to list the top ten things Navy SEALs do that will make you a badass, or brag about the awesome missions I've been on.

Instead, I offer a *here you go* book: a gathering of ideals and practices observed over the years that I believe define success and govern one's ability to navigate uncertainty, whether it is as an individual, a small team, or an organization—ideals and practices that, when actualized simultaneously, create what I consider to be *organizational fitness* (more on this concept in "Organizational Fitness").

Writing a book about the Teams was never an aspiration of mine, as I don't believe in broadcasting one's profession, but that's not the purpose of my intent here, either. To share knowledge is to serve others; to withhold it—despite any unwritten rule—is to serve oneself. To reserve insight for oneself would be criminal, as it is a purely selfish means of improving one's own self worth at the cost of others'. Knowledge-hoarding is a major pet peeve of mine—right up there with arrogance and slow drivers—as it is typically reserved for people who want to be the hero and whose ego leads the way, but obstructs everybody else's. In a world of high-performing— and highly demanding—organizations, there is no place for ego. Results come from trust, attitude, and a shared purpose.

I did minimal research for this book because I didn't need corroboration. I lived it. There are no numbers to backup the premises and I interviewed no one. Rather, the contents herein are based upon the personal experiences I have had from thirteen years in the Navy at the highest level, as well as my experiences both as a business consultant and in the private sector.

Hopefully, the insights in this book will serve you well. Even if all you take away from here is a sentence, chapter, or concept, I want it to create value for you.

Included are operational anecdotes, not for entertainment purposes, but to illustrate examples for the simple fact that special operations forces (SOF) have unique experiences to share that can help people, teams, and organizations adapt to change and become *better*. The Teams take a group of individuals, filter out the weak-minded, chip away the rough edges of those who choose to endure, and sculpt them into people who can find a solution for anything. SEAL training prepares the individual for *anything*, and this perspective in itself is something that can be adopted by both organizations and individuals who want to improve performance.

This book attempts to show how.

Organizational Fitness

The one certainty of chaos is that it is, by its very nature, uncertain. While finding success in a chaotic situation may seem to be at best an improbability and at worst an impossibility, I learned through my time in the SEAL Teams that there is method to this madness. As SEALs-in-training and on combat missions, we were thrown into every challenging situation imaginable; never knowing what to expect, and under pressure from ongoing change, we learned quickly to be ready for anything at a moment's notice. To bear the brunt of such an undefined workload requires the physical, mental, emotional, and spiritual faculties that either help or hinder success. More than anything, it requires balance among them all.

Without the emotional tolerance for stress and the mental capacity to solve problems under duress, it's more likely that your next large-scale negotiation or board presentation will be subpar. This is exactly why navigating uncertainty requires balance, because the more intangibles at your disposal, the wider your knowledge base to *create* certainty—or something that creates value for you.

fitness |'fit•nis|

noun

- *The quality of being suitable to fulfill a particular role or task*

- *The aptitude of somebody or something to fill a particular purpose*

- *To maintain or increase its numbers in succeeding generations*

I used to think that being *fit* simply meant to be an active runner, swimmer, or bodybuilder, but it doesn't. There's a broader definition of *fitness* that applies to the organization here. While any sort of exercise is certainly healthy, being truly *fit* means something else. If you ask a runner if she is fit, she will likely answer, "Yes, I run!" But if you ask a swimmer the same question he'll respond, "Yes, I swim!" Individual fitness means different things to different people, just like *winning* means different things to different people. What's more, a group of people has divergent definitions and interpretations of how to win both as individuals and as a team.

However, when you really look at the concept of *fitness*, the values and processes that *garner* winning are the same no matter what sport you play, because you never play alone. Whether you're a writer, painter, business executive, or a Navy SEAL, the performance of one activity is typically influenced by the collection of many. Nobody achieves elite status alone.

Organizational fitness is a function of multiple factors: a company's collective performance and how well they respond to an employee's need for meaningful work, how much opportunity exists for personal and professional growth, how well different corporate functions fuse together to share the same purpose, and the difference you make as a leader.

Fitness and health are not the same. You can have low cholesterol, no physical ailments, and be considered healthy, but still not be able to climb stairs because your fitness level isn't up to par. Conversely, if you are indeed fit and can perform a wide array of exercises, then a healthy body and mind are the byproducts. Fitness connotes the ability to deliver, to perform, and to execute. One may be healthy while living a relatively sedentary lifestyle, but not fit.

Companies are no different. The healthy ones have a great culture where people enjoy working, but at the end of the day, the company lacks execution. It lags behind in the marketplace or does not satiate employees' needs for growth. As a result, companies that are merely "healthy" lose market share and/or talent.

It's no secret that to wield optimal performance from an employee, he or she needs a balance of formal education and practical job-related experience, but also personal fulfillment, meaningful relationships, and opportunities to contribute and grow. (See "Sports Snapshot" below.)

However, with the rapidly changing environment that pulls business toward greater uncertainty every day, companies, in their need to stay relevant, fight the current by instituting longer workdays, investing in more analysis, and demanding more from their employees overall.

Sports Snapshot

Before sport science became a field of study, athletes and coaches trained in a linear fashion. That is, they believed that to become better they just needed to improve one's physical capacity by working harder, putting in longer hours, honing their technique, and competing more often.

Over the years, however, science improved. Discoveries in human performance were made that suggested the opposite: too much focus on one particular "silo" of training led to faster athlete burnout and actually inhibited performance.

What sport science discovered was this: for an athlete to perform optimally, he or she requires a multidimensional training regimen. That is, the physical performance associated with top-tier athletes entails not just role-specific training (i.e. sprinters sprinting, weight lifters lifting) but also nutrition, mental fortitude, sport psychology, biomechanics, economy of motion, and rest and recovery. If an athlete only has one piece of this so-called "performance puzzle," then his or her overall performance will never reach an optimal state. To perform optimally physically, one must also possess the mental, emotional, and spiritual faculties to face hardship, endure difficulty, become motivated even when not, and ceaselessly pursue a higher purpose that drives him or her to continually improve.

Now, if we take this sport-specific example of multidimensionality and apply it to one's everyday life, team, or company, what changes?

Nothing. The same multifaceted approach to performance—the balance of physical, mental, emotional, and spiritual capacities—still exists.

In other words: the typical organizational response to chaos is to become more *efficient*—to improve productivity—and the byproduct is increased stress for each and every employee. Greater stress levels lead to toxic environments, impatience, communicative challenges, and short-term focus—the very antithesis of superior performance. Under this scenario, the work-life balance unfavorably comes to lean toward work, and as a result, the company's employees suffer. Their personal reservoirs of emotional and spiritual fulfillment, for example, get depleted and refilled with unnecessary stress. Their career life expectancy becomes a time fuse, and the countdown begins until that person explodes.

The challenge, though, is in combating these types of knee-jerk reactions that arise when uncertainty presents itself. The normal response is to fight chaos with chaos by working *harder* in hopes of improved returns. What really happens in these situations, however, is the proliferation of chaos. In response to the uncertainty "out there," the busy worker bees *inside* the organization work more frantically, thus increasing the chaos "in there." Then, as a means of reducing the amount of uncertainty, people dig deeper into the weeds, analyzing more and scrutinizing everything in hopes of making the "best" decision. What results is analysis paralysis: seemingly endless meetings that adjourn with no one left in any better a position than the one they were in when they started.

The secret is to keep the performance capacities (physical, mental, emotional, spiritual) fulfilled, as doing so sustains energy levels *to* perform, *to* adapt, and *to* lead. By meeting the threshold of uncertainty posed by Murphy (of Murphy's Law) with the four pillars of performance, we can chip away at the daily challenges that arise and slap them in the face—hard.

Whether it's the SEAL Teams or business, every organization requires a broad spectrum of effort—the product of physical capability, mental capacity, emotional endurance, and spiritual enlightenment—to work through adversity. One must possess both "the skill and the will" to operate in any environment at any time for an indefinite period whenever a new threat (read: competitor) emerges. Therefore, when a person is *fit*, it means that his or her potential is limitless such that this hypothetical individual could run, swim, lift weights, move their body weight, or demonstrate flexibility anywhere, at any time. In the business sense, a *fit* individual understands the current trends affecting each department and the purpose of the organization such that he can make sales decisions even outside his field of specialty because he has the know-how and know-why to perform across multiple sectors, industries, and modalities.

In the SEALs, this concept of fitness has both deep and broad impacts upon performance. Sure, being physically fit enough just to get to some of the targets we pursue is more than half the battle—that's the physical part. Once we're facing the enemy's front door, the physical part is over; now it's time to switch into the right mental and emotional gear based on the spiritual fulfillment that drove you there. After all, it sure wasn't the handsome paycheck that attracted you.

The skill and will to span such a broad spectrum of abilities rests upon what I call the 4 Pillars of Performance, as depicted in the following image:

4 Pillars of Performance	Area to Improve
Physical	Habits, health, rest, nutrition
Mental	Focus, mental fortitude, learning
Emotional	Passion, emotional intelligence, resilience
Spiritual	Purpose, fulfillment, visualization

However, individual fitness alone will only take you so far. There needs to be trust throughout the team that other individuals and departments are capable of carrying out the mission.

What happens if *fitness*, as defined here, is lacking? Take the example of the Olympic power lifter, who may be able to power clean three hundred pounds but can't run a mile to save her life. If the power lifter enters a triathlon, she probably won't make it through the first mile because cardiovascular endurance is not something that she trains for; it isn't specific to her mission. In other words, she fails because her focus up to this point has been myopic under one silo.

Of course, not everybody in an organization needs the same level of awareness. What does the Olympic body builder stand to gain by getting in shape to run a marathon if its not going to help her attain the ultimate goal of that gold medal in lifting? Not much. Marathon training might even detract from her main goal. But what does an organization stand to gain from its CEO, CFO, COO, and other head honchos each understanding the intricacies of one another's jobs and the ultimate goals that they're working toward? Plenty.

Similarly, employees in marketing, sales, or customer service silos are generally fit to work within *their* division because they are functionally excellent in *their* roles. Ask them something about another business function, however, and their knowledge base wanes. It's a myopic view of the company that limits decision-making, awareness, and therefore, progress.

The rest of this book is a purge of ideals and beliefs that I have both experienced as a SEAL to navigate uncertainty and seen as a coach for individuals and companies. Let's begin.

The Paradox Of Uncertainty

Getting out of the military was an easy choice for a number of reasons.

First, the challenge and excitement just weren't there anymore. You can only do the same thing for so long before becoming complacent, and chasing bad guys wasn't something I wanted to be lackadaisical about—for me or for the guys I worked with.

Second, there's an emotional toll that weighs down heavily upon each operator after constantly being "on the hook" for global threats or crises to arise.

Of course, there was also the bureaucratic BS that pervades every organization. Different leaders reacted differently to stress. Some comported themselves well and put the mission first while others *allowed* stress to impact their decision-making. I use the word "allowed" because that's just what it is: a choice to open oneself to external influences because the core self lacks the self-awareness to slap adversity in the face and say, "Get outta here. I got this."

Most of our actions at the operator level relied upon the decisions made by senior leaders, and if the decision-making process stalemated for any reason, then momentum lagged across the whole organization—as did results. When this happened—when there was an impetus for action but a lack of contextual awareness—there was only one thing us operators could do: we needed to adapt. We needed to make use of the minimal guidance we had because the problem set (i.e. the threat or crisis) wasn't going to go away, and the only way to solve it was to fill the gap.

Gaps are temporary oversights: fissures in a foundation that, without the sort of direct pressure that stops bleeding, will eventually turn into large cracks that ultimately upend the foundation and render it incompetent, unserviceable, and/or irrecoverable.

And there are gaps *everywhere* in life and in organizations—communication gaps, personal meaning and fulfillment gaps, character gaps, leadership gaps. The list goes on.

You name it, and at some point there is a gap that exists at any one of the physical, mental, emotional, or social levels that drive individual and organizational performance. Why? Because shit happens. Uncertainty unfolds.

What you relied upon to get "here" no longer works, and so you must find a new way to get "there." But, the trouble is, "there" is uncertain because it's new, so getting to a new destination requires not only the skill and will to adapt to change, but also the awareness of the need to do so.

The impetus for change, whether it be personal, professional, or organizational, is not always obvious. Filling the organizational gap requires a keen understanding of not only one's particular organizational silo or specialty but also a broad contextual awareness about yourself, how your individual skill set fits across the company's, what *you* want out of work, and how your skills and expertise support the company's mission and values.

In my special operations experience, anything and everything that we faced was situated amongst a global network of uncertainty, one that continually morphed based on the interdependency that comprised geographically dispersed terrorist cells and the rate of technological change they adopted. The faster the enemy learned our targeting methods and techniques, the faster we needed to think and act to stay ahead of the curve. What allowed us to do that was—among other things—having a clear purpose.

◆◆◆

The circumstances that people and businesses face today in terms of growth, change, and interdependence cannot be solved with the same line of thinking that got them there. There must be something new. Something revolutionary that puts your brand, your product ahead of the rest. If your business operates using the same model it has for the past five, ten, or twenty years, then it's already obsolete because the very definition of *growth* entails *change*.

The change that individuals and organizations face today is never black and white and never gives way to simple solutions. To remedy chaotic situations requires a chaotic approach, one that is nonlinear, constantly morphing, and continually sharpening its competitive edge with recurring feedback loops that build upon past experiences and lessons learned. Improvement cannot be sustained without reflection.

Chaos arises from myriad sources that stem from two origins: internal chaos rising within you, and external chaos being imposed upon you by the environment. The result of this push/pull effect is the disequilibrium that you feel in your heart, mind, body, and soul, and which manifests itself as confusion, anxiety, lack of fulfillment, or despair.

At the individual level, chaos stems from both the known and the unknown—the awareness of a particular end-state; the fear, doubt, trepidation, or lack of experience we have in a particular arena; or from the personal change we experience either as a result of learning something new or an unwanted force that's pushed upon us from the outside. Managing the chaos imposed by these influences is what separates winners from losers. Why? Because the uncertainty that you face as a human being proliferates into every corner of your life, such that *your* personal chaos gives rise to challenges in your profession, and the chaos of the workday compounds the tension felt in your personal life. Without the ability or knowledge of how to manage himself physically, mentally, emotionally, or spiritually, you fall prey to depression, despair, and general shittiness.

Types of Unknowns

There are two types of unknown factors that can spiral into chaos, what I call the "Fudge Factor" and the "Oh, Shit! Factor." The Fudge Factor refers to *known unknowns*, or things that you know exist but can't quite quantify. For example, you may leave work Monday between 5:00 and 5:30 p.m. because you know the longer you wait, the more traffic will build up. You know traffic exists but you're not sure how much, so you build in a Fudge Factor of time that's high enough to compensate for what you believe will be a worthy delay. You can estimate the delay because you *know* it's there, but you *don't know* how much or for how long.

The Oh, Shit! Factor is just the opposite: *unknown* unknowns that arise out of nowhere (i.e. the external environment) that always seem to bite you in the ass at the most inopportune time, and these are the little "pleasantries" that Murphy (of Murphy's Law infamy) likes to throw at us. Planning on going to work early but your car doesn't start? *Oh, shit!* Bought a ridiculously overpriced house because of a promised year-end bonus that never materialized? *Oh, shit!* In a firefight and your weapon jams? *Oh, shit!* You get the idea.

Whether it's the military, business, or a competitive event, every single mission, deal, or play has the possibility of failure—for uncertainties of either the Fudge or Oh, Shit! variety to occur. The question is, how do you deal with such uncertainty?

During my tenure on the SEAL Teams, every enemy situation we encountered necessitated a slightly different approach, a tweak here and a new technique there. No two targets were ever the same, and each one had its own personality, its own outcome, and its own plan for how we attacked and ultimately executed it. We could never ascertain with 100 percent certainty what the enemy's intentions were or how they would respond, simply because there were just too many variables to consider.

And you know what? Business is no different.

The Paradox of Uncertainty

Uncertainty may appear boundless—limitless—but the very absence of certainty affords an equal opportunity to create it.

Random life tests like to spring up out of nowhere at the most inopportune times—led by that guy Murphy and his damn law—as a means to test us and challenge our physical, mental, emotional, and spiritual fitness as we attempt to confront these challenges head on. Possessing a balance of physical, mental, emotional, and spiritual fortitude is what allows us to endure amidst ambiguity, tackle any challenge, and say, "I got this." The challenge, of course, is that not everybody knows how to maximize his or her potential.

I have been fortunate in my life to have seen and experienced levels of performance that some people can only dream about, human achievements that bear no scientific explanation and no quantifiable evidence to explain *how*. And it all occurred under uncertain conditions.

If you consider the phenomena of *certainty* and *uncertainty* you can see an inextricably linked marvel: the fact that one cannot exist without the other. In other words, the very lack of certainty yields a one-way path toward certainty for the simple fact that nothing can be more *un*certain than it already is. I know, this is deep, but hear me out.

Look at it this way: remember all those "F's" you received on your research papers in school? (Maybe that was just me.) Getting a big red "F" at the top of a research paper says it all (i.e. "you suck") as there was no "F" minus because you couldn't really do any worse than you already did. "Bad" is bad, "suck" is suck, there is no "badder" and you can't suck any more than you already do. The same principle applies to uncertainty. From uncertainty one doesn't become any more *un*certain. It's like hitting rock bottom—and from rock bottom, the only place left to go is up.

So, what exists with both *certainty* and *uncertainty* is an interdependent system; a world, situation, or whatever you want to call it that only occurs based on the evolution and existence of the other.

No matter what system you employ to defeat the other, there are certain principles that govern certitude in human nature. For instance, you can't have trust without honesty. Likewise, there can be no learning without humility, no selflessness without service, no innovation without disruption, no leadership without followership, and no fitness without "fatness" (kidding, but you get my point). What I'm trying to say is that each element depends on its reciprocal for two things:

1. Its existence

2. Its solution

The dichotomy that uncertainty presents, then, is both a serendipitous and deliberate opportunity to create *something* from *nothing*, to find opportunity where others see conclusion. After all, only from chaos can calmness emerge.

There is chaos we deal with as individuals, teams, and organizations; chaos that presents itself at the most inopportune times, and requires you to zig when you'd rather zag. No matter where you are, chaos finds you, and if you don't know how to deal with change as an individual or as an organization, then you get eaten, swallowed whole, and left for dead.

The alternative, of course, is to never leave the womb. Or, once you do, to revert back to your safety net immediately after you realize that the waters you're in are too cold and won't suffice.

Anybody can perform a task that he or she already knows and understands. It's when obscurity, doubt, and stress are interjected into the equation against the backdrop of survival that the creature of the unknown exposes us for *who* we are, not just *what* we know how to do.

Of course, not all chaos is bad. Nobody learns from personal successes as they do from personal failures, from what he or she *should have* done or said (or not). Just as uncertainty and change spur fear and trepidation, tackling the unknown makes you better because it forces you to call upon judgment and insight that you can use to make better decisions and navigate change next time. Let me illustrate this through the following example...

The Strategy of Movement

Consider this hypothetical situation:

You and your team of twelve are in a hellacious gunfight. Bullets are ricocheting off the rocks of the mountain slope you're on and hitting all around you. You're wondering to yourself not *if* but *when* that next enemy bullet is going to skip off a rock and lodge into your gut. Meanwhile, the guy next to you—your shooting buddy—is cracking jokes from behind cover, "Whooooh hoooo! Just like fuckin' Vietnam!" despite the fact that he's under the age of thirty.

Meanwhile, the enemy has identified your position and bullets are flying at you that elicit two responses from you, the fearless team leader. The typical first response is, "Fuck! We need to get the hell outta of here!" But it's the second response that's the real moneymaker: "Where can we go?" In other words, you begin to assess the terrain for a better position. You first begin to scan the surrounding area for alternative sources of cover because you're not going to go running into a hail of bullets without first identifying the next safe position to move *to*. You want to make sure that another—better—vantage point does, in fact, exist before you order the team to move.

Once you decide upon the next best place to run for protection, you determine if the cover itself is viable for its intended purpose, which is complete tactical superiority over the enemy. *Will that tree serve the purpose that I need of stopping bullets? I haven't exercised lately, so maybe I should find a tree with a wider base.* If the area in question will not do what you want it to, then you need to keep looking.

But, if it is worthy of protecting your now puckered-up backside, then you need to pinpoint the right time *to* move, *to* change. When the opportunity presents itself, you make a deliberate decision to get up with your team, shoot back at the enemy while screaming a loud, Rambo-like "AAAAAHHHHHHHH!" and then run like hell toward your newfound sanctuary. Once there, you discover that this new piece of cover really only offers a fresh perspective in one of four ways:

1. It provides both cover *and* a fresh angle of attack on your enemy that will enable you to protect yourself, gain perspective, and win the fight.

2. It offers mediocre protection and partial exposure (at this point, you're just prolonging the nightmare).

3. It serves as a great defense but obstructs all lanes of visibility, therefore hindering your situational awareness and ability to respond.

4. It is actually a bush and bushes do not stop bullets. It fails miserably and you die.

The Lesson

The bottom line is, if you have to move in a firefight, the marketplace, or a job role, you do so for one main reason: to strategically improve the position of your team or organization. Any discomfort, whether it be physical, mental, emotional, or spiritual, is secondary. If you aren't experiencing discomfort, trepidation, or failure, then you're doing something that will bring about far graver consequences: you're trying to avoid it altogether.

In the hypothetical gunfight scenario, change only occurs when its significance has garnered the shared attention of everyone involved. You don't just move because the leader told you to. You change position because there is meaning and purpose associated with the behavior *to* move.

Failure can't be out-thought, out-strategized or out-worked. It's an element of uncertainty that appears unexpectedly and challenges you to reveal the real *you* through new circumstance.

To bounce back from failure and change for the better requires effort, courage, and the tenacity to see things through—all performance-based criteria that will be covered in upcoming chapters—but the risk of *not* changing far outweighs the temporary discomfort of the change itself.

The purpose of *moving* is to gain the high ground; to adapt amidst a changing threat toward a new situation based upon a new stimulus and thus create new meaning. However, your *ability* to move—to create value— depends on the people with whom you work, their individual and team-based competencies, their internal drivers for excellence, and their support network. This is where performance and leadership come into play.

Continuing with the above hypothetical situation, the first goal of the leader is to make sure that everybody is shooting in the right direction, and toward the same end-state such that everybody's efforts align toward the same purpose. There are a few assumptions made in this statement of "everybody is shooting in the right direction" that are important to highlight here. When people, teams, or companies share the same purpose it is presumed that:

1. **Communication is clear.** There is no ambiguity as to whom the enemy or competitor is, their position, and what resources they are employing against you. Every employee must be able to identify the battle because if you know your enemy, then you know how to defeat him. It's when you don't necessarily know your enemy intimately enough that the unforeseen arises and takes a bite out of your ass.

2. **The team is working in alignment.** The muzzle of each team member's rifle must be pointed in the same direction to maximize potential, reduce wasted efforts, and share the same purpose. Whether you are in a gunfight, a pricing war, or a product battle,

every second you lose is three more seconds you now need to advance—one second to collect yourself, one second to catch up, and another to get ahead.

3. **"Winning" has been defined.** There is no confusion about what success looks like, and everybody is on the same page to get there.

4. **Operating environment is understood before moving.** At some point, one side will have to turn the page and gain higher ground, conduct a flanking maneuver, or create some sort of change in an effort to tip the scale in their favor. A systemic understanding of the competitive landscape allows you to beat the enemy to the metaphorical high ground.

5. **Skill and performance standards exist.** Of course, if you want your top sniper to take the shot or your number one negotiator to land your next deal, it is *expected* that he or she will do so. It's an ungrateful responsibility, but one for which physical, mental, and emotional performance demands require a standard of excellence.

Once the team is aligned and shooting in the right direction, you will need to relocate and create a new formation since the enemy already knows your current position. So, what do you do? You change. You adapt and repurpose the team in such a way that the right people fall into the right places and you have the right *fit*. This also entails removing the wrong people (although not in the middle of a firefight), which only comes after you identify the performance-based skills (i.e. behaviors) that each member brings to the table and how they help or hinder your team's objectives.

Meanwhile, back in the gunfight, your team's effectiveness is decreasing by the second, so you want to keep a heavy volley of fire on the enemy to keep him suppressed. In other words, you don't want any lulls in the exchange of fire. To do this, the heavy weapons guys (.60 gunners) need to "sing" with each other at a rhythmic pace such that only one heavy weapon is firing at a time. If both fire, then you run the risk of both your heavy weapons running out of ammo simultaneously and the team revealing itself for the smaller, inferior force they really are. A constant volley of heavy fire deceivingly portrays yourselves as resourcefully superior and helps you appear much larger than the smaller force you are. There needs to be somebody with an overall view of the battlefield that can see and anticipate threats before they arrive and before they make your team obsolete. This is the essence of communication—to have complete awareness of the battlefield/industry such that every contributing member/department has the right information to make decisions. This is also the essence of effective leadership.

Shoot, Move, Communicate

We have a saying on the Teams: "Shoot, move, communicate." It's the essence of how we function together, and the lessons of "shoot, move, communicate" carry over to the business world. *Shooting* is a very technical skill that requires a complete understanding of the fundamentals (body positioning, breathing, trigger squeeze, and follow-through), and environmental factors (wind direction and sun position). Together, they all contribute to the myriad sources of information that you must consider to make the right decision, and pull that trigger at the most opportune time so that the bullet can find a home. To shoot is to make a decision based on a confluence of information. To actually pull the trigger is to take action, to lead, and to create value for others that inspires behavior.

Now, the only way to advance your performance from beginner to intermediate to advanced (to badass) is to not only grasp the fundamentals, but to *apply* them. Every. Single. Day. This requires not only incredible amounts of discipline, focus, self-awareness, and social awareness, but also the ability to harness and collectively apply them through one's physical, mental, emotional, and spiritual capacities. All of these things together determine *performance*.

While *shooting* is performance-based criteria that defines a SEAL's action, *moving* is our adaptation—our ability to change based on a need. This could take the form of physical adaptation (changing locations in a firefight, for example), personal adaptation (changing opinions or behaviors), or organizational restructuring (changing organizational culture or strategy). Whatever the impetus or the type of movement, the one constant is that to move is to learn, as you shift from what you *once knew* to be right into the unchartered territory that you now believe to be the *new* right. Humility is fundamental here, too, as it's what enables you to release your previously held mental models and move forward.

Finally, there's *communicate*. *Communication* is more than just the who, what, or why of a message. To communicate effectively entails a "we, not me" focus, and it is what inspires the action of the aforementioned elements. You will see the principle of communication revisited again and again throughout the stories in this book, for knowledge sharing is the lifeblood of any individual, team, or organization. To communicate effectively is not only to fulfill an obligation, but also to be a good team member; to be proactive and share anticipatory situations before they unfold so as to build context among the team. It is also what fuels strong leadership, another cornerstone of SEAL-style performance.

From the hypothetical gunfight scenario above, you can see that a well-developed plan means little in the face of bullets and suicide bombers. It requires comprehensive skill and insurmountable will on behalf of every team member to turn that well-developed plan into a well-executed mission and realize it in the face of the unknown. A lack of physical competence to perform or learn a new skill, for instance, does nothing to build one's confidence, which falls under both mental and emotional capacities. As a mental capacity, confidence comes in the form of self-talk, positive affirmations that in turn *build* one's emotional capacity. Similarly, for the emotional component, self-confidence helps us *feel* more competent because, by very definition, we know we can rely on ourselves when given a task that we know well. Needless to say, you can see how the four pillars are all intertwined together and inextricably linked.

The premise here is two things. First, whichever side can shoot, move, and communicate together, faster is the one that will win the fight. The critical component here—of shooting, moving, and communicating—is ensuring you're doing so effectively. Shooting more bullets, communicating more often, or moving in the wrong direction are no good without a meaningful purpose and the skill and will to pursue it. Look at it this way: as a rule of thumb, shooting without communicating the direction in which your muzzle is aimed while bullets are flying is never a good idea. Similarly, you would never just *move*—effectively—from point A to point B in a gunfight, merger, or negotiation without communicating your current position or your intended destination.

The second premise is that no single component achieves success alone. Shooting, moving, and communicating is a *system* of interrelated parts that govern and guide oneself and one's team or organization toward success.

To employ any faction independently would be an effort in futility, for it would have detrimental and/or insignificant impacts—similar to making a strategic company decision without telling anybody.

Key Takeaways

To *shoot, move*, and *communicate* in the SEAL Teams is to *perform, adapt,* and *lead* in the private sector. However, before undergoing any sort of change, you must choose the right time to adjust: too early or too late could be fateful. Thus, the significance in understanding your enemy, the operating environment, and the competencies of your team all contribute to how fast you and your organization can seize the opportunity and stay competitive.

Decisiveness, the skill and will to learn and adapt, and a shared understanding of the environment are what enable high-performing organizations to sustain high performance. But it starts with the individual.

As you can see, the three elements that made us successful on the battlefield—*shoot, move, communicate*—are the same principles and behaviors that make you and your business successful in the boardroom: *performance, adaptability, leadership*. What's more is they can operate linearly or dynamically—in sequence or not—since each one complements the others, and that's what the next chapter is about.

Performance and The PAL Model©

The paradox seems to be, as Socrates demonstrated long ago, that the truly free individual is free only to the extent of his own self-mastery [w]hile those who will not govern themselves are condemned to find masters to govern over them.

—Steven Pressfield, *The War of Art*

There are certain slogans that are drilled into our heads throughout the course of BUD/S that SEALs learn to live by: "The only easy day was yesterday," "Earn your Trident every day," "It pays to be a winner." These sayings serve to remind us of who we are and the shared purpose that binds us. *Shoot, move, and communicate* is the simplest and most fundamental way of explaining how SEALs work together. It sounds basic, but it's a winning formula with catastrophic implications if, at any point, the system breaks down.

Now, as I explained at the end of the previous chapter, what most people don't realize is that anyone from any walk of life can borrow the SEALs' dynamic for success; it just needs a little bit of translating for the private sector. That's where the PAL Model© comes in.

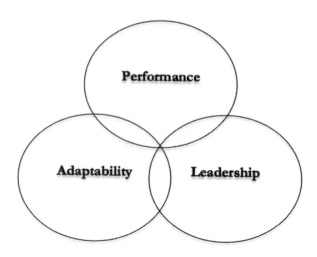

The PAL Model© refers to the way in which any team—whether at work, on the athletic field, or even at home—can borrow this dynamic from the SEALs and apply it to their own efforts toward success. Shooting is the skill that embodies the SEALs' efficacy on the battlefield; it's the most fundamental of the skills that we need to perform, but off the battlefield, it's all about performance (the "P" in PAL). Does each and every member of your team have the skillset in place that is needed to advance the team's collective cause? That's the performance piece.

Similarly, as I demonstrated in the previous chapter's firefight illustration, a SEAL's ability to survive in combat hinges upon his—and his team's—ability to move. In the civilian world, what we're talking about is adaptability (the "A" in PAL). Adaptability is what enables any team to tackle the unknown and strategically improve their position at a moment's notice.

Finally, there's *communicate*. If a SEAL decides to move in battle but that message doesn't come across to his brothers and they don't move together with shared purpose, it could result in his, or worse, his team's, demise. If this happens it's game over, with no chance to try again. Off the battlefield, communication translates to the "L" piece of PAL: leadership. Without effective leadership in any situation, communication breaks down and things rapidly spin out of control.

Before moving on, I'd like to make one small note about performance. While the term definitely connotes performance of the physical sort, it is critical not to overlook the mental, emotional, and spiritual pieces, which *comprise* the larger puzzle of performance. All four elements—physical, mental, emotional, spiritual—contribute to one's daily living, how he or she feels, and, ultimately, how he or she *performs*. Varying levels of each are called upon based on the task at hand, but the capacity of each still exists.

No matter your objectives, goals, or pursuits, the mental piece is what sets the wheels in motion *to* execute or *to* pursue said goals; it is what encapsulates *intent*, which is the essential building block to thought, emotion, and behavior.

The Mental Piece

While I could write another book on mental toughness alone, that's not what this next section is about. The purpose of the next section is to share with you specific aspects of mental toughness that helped me navigate uncertainty. While this is certainly not the end-all-be-all list for finding solutions, it is what has worked for me and what I'll share with you.

Mihaly Csikszentmihalyi, in his bestselling book *Flow: The Psychology of Optimal Performance*, says that to achieve optimal performance, one must merge behavior with intent. Doing so undoubtedly requires a laser-like focus that not many people *choose* or *know how* to employ. Common office distractions such as calendar reminders, cell phones, background noise, and that annoying email inbox chime all serve as momentary distractions that divert your attention away from the task at hand and, as a result, make your output sub-optimal. To sustain superior performance, you need a mental gear shift of intent and focus. This gives you the awareness to know when to downshift to first gear or even "park," and when to put the pedal to the metal and shift into high gear.

How PAL© Works

Before sport science became a widely known field of study, athletes and coaches trained in a linear fashion. In the old way of thinking, the belief was that, in order to become better, an athlete just needed to improve his or her physical capacity by working harder, putting in longer hours, honing their technique, and competing more often.

Over the years, however, discoveries in human performance were made that suggested that the opposite was actually true: too *much* focus on one particular "silo" of training led to faster athlete burnout and actually *inhibited* performance.

What sport science discovered was this: for an athlete to perform optimally, he or she requires a multidimensional training regimen. That is, the physical performance associated with top-tier athletes entails not just role-specific training (i.e. sprinters sprinting, weight lifters lifting) but also nutrition, mental fortitude, sport psychology, biomechanics, economy of motion, and rest and recovery. If an athlete only has one piece of this so-called "performance puzzle," then his or her overall performance will never reach an optimal state. To perform optimally *physically,* one must also possess the proper faculties to face hardship, endure difficulty, become motivated, and ceaselessly pursue a higher purpose that drives him or her to continually improve.

Now, if we take this sport-specific example of multidimensionality and apply it to one's everyday life, team, or company, what changes?

Nothing. The same multifaceted approach to performance—the balance of physical, mental, emotional, and spiritual capacities—still exists, and it is the basis of performance.

The "P" in PAL: Performance

For the PAL Model©, I consider Performance to encompass four life capacities, referred to hereafter as "the four pillars," that constitute human output: physical, mental, emotional, and spiritual. Collectively, the four pillars all comprise the full makeup of one's being and are critical to navigating chaos when chaos arrives—as it always will.

In the PAL Model©, performance corresponds to the *shoot* component of *shoot, move, communicate.* The physical, mental, emotional, and spiritual aspects that go into squeezing that trigger and ensuring that the bullet finds its intended target are critical, but so are the internal and external awareness that the shooter must have to ensure his bullet finds the right home. Believe it or not, sending a one-inch projectile across three hundred yards is no easy feat, let alone eight hundred yards or one thousand. There are significant steps one must take to get and stay "in the zone," and that's what the performance section will cover.

There are many points of performance when it comes to shooting, which is why *performance* is the foundation upon which PAL© is built. The physical positioning of the shooter is key as his (or her) body is the foundation that affords the greater certainty that serves as the foundation of a solid shot. The mental aspect of focus and concentration supersedes all else because without mental focus all else—the discomforts of life—pour into the mind and overwhelm it. Every distraction in nature wants to throw your bullet off its intended path, and the amount of mental focus it takes to ignore those seemingly tiny disturbances is significant—but no more significant than what it takes to perform optimally in business.

Next is the emotional piece, which is the feeling of comfort, control and acceptance that one must have before and after taking the shot. There can be no second-guessing, no hesitancy, only the willingness to look (and move) forward to the next objective.

Finally, the spiritual piece is where purpose and passion play in, as they are what provide fulfillment and meaning to your actions. Being spiritually content enables you to continue taking more shots and never doubt or second-guess yourself. The convergence of these four elements is where certainty lies. The key, obviously, is learning how to balance the four amongst a world of constant change and disruption.

The "A" in PAL: Adaptability

The need to adapt comes from the uncertainty of a situation that is both a challenge and an opportunity. The uncertainty that springs up out of nowhere acts as a defining moment to test your skill and will, your spirit and motivation. What separates those who stay relevant from those who don't is their willingness to adapt.

Adaptability allows you to respond immediately and intelligently to constant change so as to seize opportunity where others might see obstruction. Adaptive capacity also facilitates forward momentum because it lessens the need to have to stop what you're doing to review what happened. Instead, you're in a fluid, dynamic state that continually "reads and reacts" to problems as they arise.

The late Warren Bennis, widely considered a pioneer of the study of leadership, once described people with adaptive capacity as individuals who:

...may struggle in the crucibles they encounter, but they don't become stuck in or defined by them. They learn important lessons, including new skills that allow them to move on to new levels of achievement and new levels of learning. This ongoing process of challenge, adaptation, and learning prepares the individual for the next crucible, where the process is repeated. Whenever significant new problems are encountered and dealt with adaptively, new levels of competence are achieved, better preparing the individual for the next challenge.

Adaptability refers to an organism's ability to stay relevant amidst change; to adjust to new conditions based on a compelling impetus to do so. To stay current—to do away with the old and adapt to the new—requires the skill and will to do so, and this change stems from performance-based criteria mentioned above. In the scientific world, adaptability depends on two things: self-renewal and self-organization.

- *Self-renewal refers to your skill and will to reexamine and ultimately reset any emotional "hiccups" that may have caused your values and subsequent behavior to derail. It is your ability to both learn and unlearn.*

- *Self-organization refers to individual and/or group behavior without direction from external authorities. For instance, when an eighth grade teacher leaves her classroom, the students have two choices: they can incite chaos and behave poorly, or they can maintain their composure and align their behavior to the teacher's objectives. In either instance, the students guide their behavior based on the understanding and mutual agreement they all share. The students' abilities to self organize, then, isn't dependent upon an external force to guide them along.*

What this means is that if an organism or system can self-organize, then, by definition it can also adapt. If the hypothetical students above lacked self-organization, then they would've needed guidance from an external authority figure. But they didn't. Instead, they *moved* from a setting under which their teacher measured their performance, to one where their performance was measured by their own willingness to perform—they *un*learned and relearned.

Furthermore, if such a self-organized group of students can create "something from nothing," then such an act also speaks to the emergence of leadership.

The "L" in PAL: Leadership

Contrary to common belief, leadership is not indicative of one's position, status, or authority. Just because you are defined as a "leader" through semantics, doesn't mean you know how to lead. Leadership does not fall upon the shoulders of the person with the loudest voice, but rather the individual who possesses both the character and competence that inspires others. To lead is to express oneself authentically through a display of decisions and actions that inspire others to think or act in a certain way.

Here's a quick way to test your leadership effectiveness. Ask yourself, "Will people follow me *because* of my position, or *despite* it?" If the answer is the former, sorry, but you still have work to do.

Here's how leadership unravels under the PAL Model©:

Every individual possesses the four pillars. The degree to which his or her physical, mental, emotional, and spiritual capacities are filled, however, differs as some people are more emotionally charged while others stem from a long line mental meatheads. There are two pathways here that lead to adaptability. The first is person A, whose four pillars of performance are completely satiated such that he doesn't need time to rest and renew; he's ready for greater self-actualization. Self-actualization is the practice of realizing one's potential. To the extent that his four pillars are already maxed out, however, the only possible next step is to push himself further; to change his current state and *adapt* to a new one.

Conversely, person B lacks mental fortitude and is emotionally unstable. His four pillars are not maximized which, by simple definition, indicates that adaptability is inherent given a person's intrinsic need *to* self-actualize.

The very act of adapting personifies leadership, as leadership is defined as a behavior of self-expression that creates value for oneself and/or for others.

Key Takeaways

- *The physical, mental, emotional, and spiritual capacities require fulfillment based on any motivational theory*

- *Whether you lack fulfillment in one capacity or are satiated across all four, the only possible next step is to change something in one way, shape, or form, and change entails adaptability.*

"He Fucking Shot Me!"

A man should conceive of a legitimate purpose in his heart, and set out to accomplish it. He should make this purpose the centralizing point of his thoughts. It may take the form of a spiritual ideal, or it may be a worldly object, according to his nature at the time being; but whichever it is, he should steadily focus his thought forces upon the object that he has set before him. He should make this purpose his supreme duty, and should devote himself to its attainment, not allowing his thoughts to wander away into ephemeral fancies, longings, and imaginings. This is the royal road to self-control and true concentration of thought. Even if he fails again and again to accomplish his purpose (as he necessarily must until weakness is overcome), the strength of character gained will be the measure of his true success, and this will form a new starting point for future power and triumph.

—James Allen, *As a Man Thinketh*

Efforts and courage are not enough without purpose and direction.

—John F. Kennedy

Diyala Province, Iraq 2007

I stacked up on my shooting buddy who was on the right side of the doorway. His body language told me that he was ready for a leg squeeze, which was the green light to initiate clearance. He (I'll just call him J) opened the door inward while standing on the hinge side. As the door opened, he slowly cleared the room only to see a woman run across from right to left. As the woman made her dash, the door opened more, so using the door as concealment, J bumped across to the other side so he could clear the dead space behind the door that he had not yet seen. As he moved across, I took up the side of the door where J had been and began my clearance. I swept around to the uncleared corner of the room but, before I got there, I noticed something wasn't right.

The individual we were targeting was a known al Qaeda leader within Iraq's Diyala province, which had become a recent hotbed of insurgency. Intelligence had driven our strike force to a small farmhouse in the middle of nowhere.

Peering just over the muzzle of my rifle while scanning the room, I could make something out through the corner of my eye that was unlike anything on any of the other targets we had done. There was a man-like figure in the corner and…the more I swung my muzzle toward that area… the more I realized that it was not *just* a man…but an insurgent standing there with an AK-47. He was standing there with an AK on his hip pointed at us—me, rather—just waiting to fire. At that moment, I knew he had the drop on me.

"Oh, shit!"

It's amazing how fast the brain processes context. The hundreds of thousands of hours that I had trained had ingrained in me not only habits but also judgment, and at that very instant of seeing this insurgent out of my peripheral vision, I knew that I could not swing my muzzle over to him, acquire, aim, fire, and kill him faster than he could kill me. My muscle memory knew its capabilities, and I knew that if I tried then I would lose and I would be dead.

As I tried to tuck back behind the doorframe, the unknown figure blasted off a short burst from his AK and I immediately felt the impacts both on my rifle and my chest. I remember thinking, incredulously, "He fucking shot me!" In fact, my teammates laugh now because apparently, I actually said it aloud. I was more insulted and pissed off than anything because it was difficult to comprehend the gall of this guy! Didn't he know who we were? We were SEAL Team freakin'—! That was the arrogance—and ignorance—with which I operated at the time, because I lacked the experience to know better. I did not respect the enemy or his dwelling, and I took being at "the door" for granted.

The first round hit me in the lower left corner of the front plate of my body armor—about an inch high and an inch left from blowing out my left hip, and a few inches above the Boss Baby Maker. The second 7.62 round shot off the forward pistol grip of my HK 416 where I was gripping it—in that tiny, quarter-of-an-inch area where the grip attaches to the Picatinny rail system. The third round hit the rail of my rifle, followed by another. All in all there were three bullet impacts on the rail of my gun and one on me. *Thank God for people smarter than me who can engineer this sort of protection,* I later thought to myself. Four rounds, all from approximately eight feet away, were spat from an Iraqi insurgent shooting an AK-47 shooting from his hip.

In that moment, after getting shot, I knew instantly that I had become a member of a certain club—a club that nobody else wanted to join.

It's the club of wounded soldiers.

But, unlike someone who falls down and chooses to stay down, I chose to get back up and keep going, to keep coming back for more, again and again, deployment after deployment, hardship after hardship. More importantly, so did my teammates. While I've been in some pretty nauseating circumstances, so have my brothers in arms, and *they* chose to return to the fight, too.

Meanwhile, my shooting buddy had a clear vantage point from his side of the door, where he engaged and killed the man who had just tried to kill me. I was more angry than traumatized that this guy had just tried to take my life, but I got over it pretty quickly—about twelve seconds to be exact—and continued prosecuting the target until it was secure. Once rendered safe, J and I began to tactically question the remaining inhabitants of the house in an effort to elicit any valuable information in the wake of such an assumingly traumatic event for them. It turned out that the woman who ran across the room at the beginning of our clearance was both the insurgent's cousin and wife, and she had been instructed by him to run away from his position within the room to draw our attention away from the corner from which he was planning his ambush. When asked about how she felt that we had just killed him, she just shrugged her shoulders: "Eh, he was an asshole."

◆◆◆

A number of instances in my life have driven home the fact that purpose is a primary motivator for success, and it's because of the passion and fulfillment that it yields. If the meaning and satisfaction that I derived from the job were not clearly defined after the *first time* I was shot, then I would have put down my rifle and found a desk job, or hung up my parachute after my first parachute malfunction (more on that later). But I didn't. Instead,

I was *pulled* back toward the pack for another round. I had a purpose to serve and my thirst for more just wasn't quenched yet.

When one's job role increases in meaning, it becomes easier to endure amidst challenge and adversity for the simple fact that *fear conquers fear.*

Here's what I mean.

To be purposeful and passionate about what you do does not mean you live a life full of rainbows and unicorns. There are challenges, letdowns, and tumultuous times. But when you're passionate about your work, you become more committed and you proactively seek more ways to engage and find solutions—because if you don't, then a heavy weight of guilt rests upon your shoulders until you do. Since you want to succeed, you're more likely to leave your circle of comfort and face conflict with others and you fear that if you don't, then that irresistible urge to quench your motivational thirst will never be fulfilled. But when you do, you discover that the harder that "thing" is the more you get out of it, and you get addicted to success. To try and fail at a task that frightens you overrides the fear of not trying at all.

Fear conquers fear.

◆◆◆

Purpose is that intangible force that summons people to *move,* and has been presented to me at multiple stages in my life across a wide range of scenarios as a means of questioning my desire and beliefs of what I held to be "right." It's based on what you value and choose to act upon, and as you gather meaning and value from those pursuits, passion forms. For any person or organization to be organizationally *fit,* employees must find meaning at work that warrants such a chase. People oftentimes join the military for an ideal because that ideal is hard to find otherwise. Companies are no different. They attract or repel talent based on the values and purposes they embody. This is one of the few times where the gray area of life dissipates and becomes black or white.

Without a direction, a mission, or a path to guide behavior, an unclear purpose leads to nowhere. Hell, just consider the types of meetings you attend in your company. How many meetings actually serve the purpose for which they're called? Personally, I like to write the purpose of the meeting on a whiteboard for all to see so that *when* conversations go off topic, we can simply refer to the purpose that brought everybody together. Making purpose clear helps keep everybody aligned and able to make mini course adjustments along the way.

The bottom line is that for purpose to find fulfillment, it needs to lead to effective action. In special warfare, the ability to shoot, move, and communicate as one fluid unit is what turns uncertainty into something palpable—which also means that it's manageable and measurable. Effectiveness comes from being grounded in what you do and why you do it; from *creating* a solution, rather than one day hoping to find the answer. There is a purpose for everything we do in specwar, and everything you do in your company. Every critical information node, meeting, job assignment, employee selection, mission set, sale, or training schedule serves a purpose. The question is: does that purpose create its intended value?

I am a firm believer in having a meaning for everything, a reason for why things happen—not framed in a spiritual or religious light, but instead understood rationally. Without a belief to point us toward "right," the temptation to yield to inferior rationale grows stronger. If this snowball of temptation grows too large, it becomes easier to make decisions based upon emotion rather than reason. Without purpose, the drive to sustain superior performance dwindles away, because there is no significance for what you do or why you do it. You can only go so far on self-discipline or willpower alone because, at some point, you just get tired of *pushing* yourself. The metaphorical-emotional gas tank eventually runs empty. To be purpose-driven, however, is to be *pulled* in a direction that ignites the craving for even more discoveries, and is a theme that will be revisited often throughout this book.

For SOF, our purpose is to affect change. We do so by carrying out the strategy that allows us to constantly adapt our capabilities and win in uncertain environments. Dead bad guys just happen to be the result.

Purpose brings meaningfulness that fuels the fire for even greater intellectual curiosity and Sustained Superior Performance (SSP). I like to define SSP as *steadfast execution amidst frequent uncertainty*. People who can perform in the face of ambiguity—those who can conceptually build a mental and emotional bridge and safely maneuver across it without setback—are the ones who ultimately discover their *high performance* status.

The principles outlined in this book are what I believe lead to success whether on the battlefield or in the boardroom. Identifying a purpose and being passionate about what you do; possessing the character and competence to trust and be trusted; having a strong family or support network; and being humble enough to shut up, learn, and serve others all combine to create what I believe to be an indestructible human machine. A person who is highly motivated to learn and has the support network to do so is a dangerous adversary, because there is nothing over which the heart and mind cannot collectively triumph. Fighting with values and principles will always outweigh weapons and munitions. A rifle will run out of bullets, but the source that fuels an individual's reason for being will never cease. Hell, look at Afghanistan. No single nation has ever conquered that godforsaken country despite technological and military advantages up the behind. I have seen the aforementioned sense of purpose firsthand by means of suicide bombers and barricaded shooters who *knew* they were going to die, but just didn't care, because their *sole mission in life* was to take us with them. It is extremely difficult to defend against an enemy who only cares about one thing and will do *anything* to achieve it, including martyr himself.

The above elements are by no means the only components that contribute to sustained superior performance; they are simply what I have found to create meaningfulness, passion in life, and individual and team success.

High-demanding jobs demand high performance ideals, and to be considered tier one in any industry requires tier one people. Jobs that require you to constantly travel and be away from your family, to face danger more than the average Joe, or to deal with significant financial risk necessitate more than just a step-by-step process of *how* to do these things. Replicating "best practices" simply won't cut it because what works for Company A may be a horrid idea for Company B.

Purpose was the guiding light that allowed me to persevere through uncommon challenges, as purpose offers clarity on what is to be expected and what is to be achieved. In no particular order, the other elements in this book helped me feel more obliged to carry on when the *power of choice* became a test against *temptation*.

Ohio State University, 1998

One of my first *how-bad-do-you-want-to-be-a-SEAL?* tests came my sophomore year in college. Every morning I would wake up at five o'clock to run four miles, then afterwards make a ridiculously oversized breakfast. My dad used to sarcastically joke that instead of opening the refrigerator door to eat, I should just stick the entire fridge between two slices of bread because it would save time. Breakfast was actually more a question of what I *didn't* eat rather than what I *did*.

I would run to the gym to run on the treadmill, which makes absolutely no sense now that I see that sentence. On this particular morning in college, though, after doing the first mile on the treadmill, I started to see black spots.

Instead of ending the workout right then and there, like a normal human being, I decided to press on. But the harder and longer I ran, the more the dark spots would intensify and the greater my vision would constrict. Finally, I had to stop. I figured that if I stopped, then the blurriness would go away, and if the blurriness went away then I'd be able to finish the workout (I never claimed to be a genius). But as I walked away, the situation just worsened. In fact, my vision disappeared, as did my balance. I found a bench to lie down on outside when, coincidentally, a medical school student happened to be walking by and noticed that something was not right with me. She called an ambulance that took me to the hospital, only to discover my blood pressure at a "healthy" sixty over forty.

Not good.

At this point, there was still no clear indication as to *why* this event occurred because sports, exercise, and healthy eating had all been significant and consistent parts of my life through that point.

Like an idiot, I told my then–SEAL recruiter about the incident and he said it would preclude me from volunteering for the SEALs, but to let the situation develop a little more, talk with the doctors, and wait to see if anything changed. All I heard, though, was, "You're fucked."

I was devastated. I had envisioned becoming a SEAL since high school, and I was now being told that my dream was impossible. The search for doctors began—intensely—and after talking with multiple MDs who tried to identify the root cause of my adverse reaction, it came down to one final heart doctor, who also happened to shatter my dreams.

This cardiologist essentially said that I could never exercise and, therefore, could definitely *never* be a Navy SEAL since the incident was clearly a heart issue as it involved elevating my heart rate. I broke down in tears right there in his office with my dad right next to me. It was embarrassing, but I couldn't control it because just a year earlier a skin irritation that prevented me from enlisting after high school had finally cleared up, and a letter from a dermatologist had cleared my entrance for the Navy. But now all those dreams were gone. In telling me "no," this heart doctor had brought me down to a reality that I didn't want to accept. He made me question my passion of how badly I wanted to go to BUD/S (Basic Underwater Demolition/SEAL training).

My mom, ever so supportive, always ingrained in me not to worry about things I could not control, and that "things will work out as they should." Her patience and optimism have carried me through to this day and have helped shape my resiliency.

Meanwhile, over the same time period of my college career, my dad had been seeing a doctor friend of his own[1], but not for medical reasons. Gwen was awesome, and incredibly supportive. She had been with me every step of the referrals, made new introductions, and she was there that day in the heart doctor's office. More importantly, she didn't believe the shit that the cardiologist was slinging.

"Listen, Jeff, I want to try one last thing. Do you remember what you ate for breakfast that day?" My eyebrows raised as the picture of a refrigerator in-between two pieces of bread passed through my mind.

"Yeah, I think so." I replied. Any shot was better than no shot, I figured.

"Okay, let's try a food allergy test and see if anything pops. I'll get you scheduled for next week. Who knows; it may open up some doors for us."

---

1   My parents were divorced

I was doubtful, but I agreed. Then, to everyone's surprise the food allergy test revealed two foods that I was allergic to: parsley and celery. Moreover, the anaphylactic reaction that occurred that day on campus was exercise-induced which meant that I could eat parsley or celery anytime but if I exercised right afterwards, then my face would blow up again and I would look like one of the creatures from the bar in the movie *Star Wars*.

Why did this happen? *Why* did I have to waste time, effort, and money in discovering something that would never affect my entrance into the Navy? My belief is that it was to instill just how important a personal mission (i.e. purpose) was, to question my desire about how badly I wanted to become a SEAL, and the extent to which I would pursue this dream. In high school, I was denied military entrance due to a skin irritation that miraculously appeared out of nowhere and then disappeared right after trying to enlist. While there was certainly sadness and depression in high school about not being able to join, in college the disappointment was tenfold. My focus on purpose—on meaning—was so deeply ingrained in me by then that no other career field was even an option. I am forever indebted to not only my parents and their support during that time, but Gwen's as well. Her support will never be forgotten.

Summary

Without a purpose to fuel your performance, success will be short-lived. Without purpose, an individual, company, or team bears no value and the superiority component of competition fizzles out.

More so, purpose comes from within. If you wait for some external force to cajole you along in the right direction, you'll always be waiting.

The bottom line is this: purpose validates your beliefs and, therefore, your actions. It supersedes fear—even if fear is that element trying to rein you back from pursuing your purpose—because it affords opportunity, which is something that nobody else can offer you except *you*.

As this book will show, one's ability to shoot, move, and communicate throughout business or life all starts with having purpose and passion for what you do. But, to sustain superior performance indefinitely, one must have purpose's sibling, passion, to *feel* the fire, as the next chapter will show.

Passion Presents Itself

Circumstance does not make the man, it reveals him.

—James Allen

Anybody can perform a task that he or she already knows and understands. It's when obscurity, doubt, and stress are interjected into the equation against the backdrop of survival that the creature of the unknown exposes us for *who* we are, not just *what* we know how to do.

The circumstances that tested me appeared on a number of different occasions, and each one seemed to question how badly I wanted to press on. Each episode created yet another façade of disbelief that deeply tested my resolve, to which I bluntly answered the call every time—at least I like to think so—and that's a question that passion answers.

Coronado, CA, April 2000: Hell Week

Despite kicking and screaming from my parents, I finally enlisted in the Navy on April 19, 2000—with a BUD/S contract. I am not going to rattle off another story from SEAL training, as there are plenty of books out there that will do just that. However, certain milestones within my BUD/S experience are important to highlight because they underline the value of passion in one's life endeavor.

The third week of BUD/S was hell week—a significant milestone in the SEAL training pipeline that separates the weak-minded from the purpose-driven. It is a tool used to select the right people. In hell week, students are cold, wet, tired, and miserable for five and a half days with a maximum of four hours of sleep the whole week. Scientists say that anything *greater than* 120 hours of sleeplessness causes permanent brain damage. Hell week is *up to* 120 hours—that's how far we like to push the envelope.

Hell week is daunting, to say the least. But it is also an incredible experience that shapes SEAL wannabes into *knowing*—not just believing—that the human mind is the most powerful weapon that anybody can possess. You learn that the only human limitations are those that you place on yourself, and that failure is only determined by where you choose to stop.

However, hell week was only the third week of training, and it didn't seem like the instructor staff had given us the secret thought-recipe to making it through yet (they weren't particularly friendly at that point in time). My question back then was, *If hell week is the third week, what the hell comes after that?*

On Saturday, or hell week *eve*, you sleep as much as possible, which really ends up being no more than normal. You eat and rest because come five o'clock Sunday evening, your new day begins, and it's going to be a looooong 120-hour day. At five o'clock Sunday evening, our class shuffled over to the BUD/S compound where we lay in tents, awaiting an unknown time at which hell week would begin. There were a few things that ran through my mind while I lay in wait for the M60 machine gun bursts to start, which was the signal from the instructors that hell week has begun, such as: *How have they (the instructor staff) prepared me for this? This week was more difficult than the first, my legs feel like anchors, and I feel like I just played a football game with no pads. How am I supposed to feel fresh? Does anyone else feel fresh? What mental tools do they have? God, this is really gonna suck.*

My mental position at the time was one of entitlement in that I expected *them* (the instructors) to give me something cognitive that would ensure success. Obviously, that wasn't the case for a number of reasons, the most important one being that nobody gives you anything you don't already have; they just offer you opportunities to unlock it from its dusty, never-been-used-before mental warchest.

Ka-booom!

Bap-bap-bap-bap-bap-bap-bap…! Explosions and automatic weapons fire sounded off.

"Get the hell outta the tents!"

"Wake up! Move your asses!" screamed the instructor staff. "Move! Move! Move!"

It was game time.

The explosions and heavy put-put-puttering of the M60 machine guns officially commenced the beginning of hell week. At that point, it was pure chaos.

All the trainees ran out of their calm, quiet tents right into pandemonium—an instantaneous shift from something so simple into something extremely complex. Instructors were yelling and throwing grenade simulators that were going off all around us; smoke, explosions, and, worst of all, water hoses were everywhere. From the moment you exited the tent until you finished five and half days later (if you made it), you were cold, wet, miserable, and tired. *The whole time.*

It was miserable. To this day, I do not get in cold water and I hate swimming. No joke.

But, as time slowly idled by that week and more and more classmates quit—guys who I thought would make it through—I began to realize that their mental weakness was a choice derived from a *temporary state* of unpleasantness. If there was one thing I learned from hell week, it was that nothing lasts forever. If you can focus on an alternate, temporary reward, then the short-term pain of *now* will dissipate, and you'll ultimately reach your long-term goal, whatever that may be. What you focus on is what you get, and I *chose* to focus on short-term, temporary wins that garnered long-term success. I did this by separating each training evolution over the course of a day into its own individual routine with its own focus, as if it were the last task to do for that day and nothing else mattered. Short-term goals act as a mental bridge toward a far-away destination (long-term goals), allowing you to not only align yourself toward your end state but also to give your mental and emotional faculties relief. Put another way, it was easier to aim toward the next meal that was just four hours away than to imagine being awake for five days straight. Plus, the thought of spending the rest of my enlistment on a ship was enough to keep myself in check. Conversely, quitters only focused on the immediate pain of what was currently in front of them.

Monday came and I wasn't feeling too tired. Then Monday night. Then Tuesday morning. By the time Tuesday afternoon rolled around, I was in Zombieland. I mentally checked out. My mind had accepted the current level of discomfort that we were enduring, and there was no way I was going anywhere except into Wednesday. Everywhere you run in hell week is with your BUD/S class, which consists of boat crews that yield five to seven individuals each. Each boat crew carries a small inflatable boat on the head of each member, anywhere and everywhere the class travels. I remember running back from chow one day with that damn boat on my head and falling asleep while running, only to wake up about forty yards ahead of the last place I remembered. The power of the human mind is truly amazing.

And then, that night, it happened.

Every few hours, students received medical checks to ensure they're not doing any grave harm to their bodies. Of course, "grave" is a subjective term. At this point, though, having made it this far into hell week, students were more inclined to hide their injuries for fear of being "rolled back" to another class, and having to start over after their injuries healed.

Well, I pulled the short straw this particular med check.

On Tuesday night of hell week I was rolled out of the class for a femoral stress fracture, and all hopes and dreams of becoming a SEAL were lost.

You gotta be fucking kidding me! I thought to myself. I was devastated. It was absolute emotional turmoil thinking that my life's purpose was not going to be realized. I will never forget sitting in the chow hall on Wednesday morning, just hours after being rolled back, and seeing my class—and even worse, my boat crew—filter through the chow line like a pack of wild dogs scavenging the only food left. They looked like zombies. I had just slept for the first time since Sunday, which helped settle my mind, but they had not. I could see the difference in how I felt and how the class looked even after just a few hours of sleep. The thought that my career, life objective, and personal being were out of my control was incredibly challenging to face. For a long time after being rolled back I always wondered, "*Why?*"

Why did this happen? I know I can make it through BUD/S.

What am I supposed to learn or gain from this setback?

It was not until years later—after a few more incidents—that the answer was revealed, as the upcoming chapters will show.

Lessons Learned

Serving others who believe in service is important to me, as it is what has compelled me to pursue the achievements in life, and to write this damn book. But the next sequence of events turned out to be a little more stressful.

Everything that occurs in life, both good and bad, forces you to learn and shapes who you are. My dad once told me that the difference between *you* now and *you* twenty years from now is the places you'll go and the people you'll meet. Boy, was he right.

The guys I met in my new BUD/S class were incredible, and are still my closest friends and the best people I will ever know. Hell, one became my brother-in-law, which is a whole other story. Another close friend (and his unfortunate death) set me on my path to where I am now—writing about purpose and service because that is why I believe he existed and why our friendship was so tight.

To be passionate about something is to believe in the meaning that you anticipate *it* to deliver—whatever that meaning is—and to possess an intense desire to continue into the fray. Purpose and passion are two opposing forces that seem to work synergistically or individually, either on your behalf or against your best interest. Passion *drives* you, whereas purpose *pulls* you. Purpose can tug you along in its direction when passion subsides and thus allow you to endure amidst uncertainty, conflict, or fear. Purpose and passion can both be your friends and your fatal enemies.

To be passionate about something is to wake up everyday with the intention of living life to the fullest because your passion *drives* you; it offers constant and immediate feedback that you are on the right path— *your* path—toward attaining your objective, until you finally get there and your potential is realized.

When you're passionate about your job, your life, and your relationships, you become more committed and proactively seek more ways *to* learn, engage, and find solutions. Because your purpose fuels you, you are more willing to face conflict or potential failure—again—because you value the learning opportunities that evolve either way.

Currituck, NC 2008: "Damnit, not again!"

Currituck is about a forty-five minute drive from Dam Neck, Virginia, where I was based, so oftentimes we would rent a plane and schedule a few days to go down to the airfield and practice high altitude, low opening (HALO) and high altitude, high opening (HAHO) parachute jumps. We would go through the jumpmaster brief that covered the sequence of events for the day, identify the roles and responsibilities for all personnel involved, and review the mishap procedures for parachute malfunctions—something that I always paid attention to because I never considered myself a stellar jumper.

After the brief, we all donned our parachutes, crammed into the plane, and sat "nut to butt," as Navy guys supposedly like to do, and climbed to fifteen thousand feet for a HALO jump. We dove out and performed the sexy maneuvers in the air that we had planned. At about five thousand feet, we separated so as to create distance between both our parachutes and ourselves, to avoid bunching up on each other and causing traffic collisions in the air. You want space between you and other jumpers when you "throw out," or pull the parachute's ripcord, because the last thing you want is to be right on top of somebody after their parachute inflates. The more space you have to maneuver, the better.

After clearing my airspace for other jumpers, I went to pull the ripcord, break the burble to allow my 'chute to catch wind, and proceeded to keep falling…and falling…and falling. Normally, when the ripcord is pulled, the parachute deploys and inflates within a few seconds. But these few seconds had passed without the expected jolt, and I realized there was a significant problem.

My parachute didn't open.

Fuuuuck!

Not only did my parachute not open, but there wasn't *any indication* whatsoever that it was even close to opening. This was not a good thing.

I glanced back over my shoulder to try and identify the problem. *Holy shit, I got a pack closure.* A pack closure is a complete parachute malfunction in which the pack tray that holds the parachute remains closed. It is the absolute worst failure that can happen and perfectly fitting for my sort of luck.

As I continued falling and the trees below me became larger and larger, I immediately went to the emergency procedures (EPs) outlined in the jumpmaster brief. EPs are the procedures a jumper executes if the main parachute fails to operate, and are identified by two different colored tabs on a jumper's chest harness. Pulling one tab will activate a severing mechanism inside the pack tray to "cut away" the main chute, while pulling the other tab will activate the reserve chute. It's important to do them in sequence so you don't inflate your reserve parachute into the main and cause even more problems for yourself. There is actually a technical term for this sort of malfunction, it's called: "Getting fucked."

From the time it took me to initiate emergency procedures to the time my reserve parachute actually opened, a lot of things passed through my mind. The first was, "*Holy-shit-I'm-gonna-die.*" The second was the fact that I was falling over a wooded area with dense trees, and so naturally the scene from *First Blood* popped into my mind, when Sylvester Stallone was hanging on the face of a cliff in an attempt to outrun the cops until he decided to jump off the cliff and into a cluster of treetops, with the hopes of the branches breaking his fall.

Of course Rambo survived because, well, he was Rambo. But I was Jeff Boss, and I was plummeting to the earth at 170 mph from 15,000 feet. Needless to say, I wasn't going to bounce. I remember feeling my heart pound through my chest because the reserve chute was supposed to open instantaneously but, of course, it didn't. It probably opened at about 1,500 feet and when it did, I felt like I had just resurfaced from underwater to breathe fresh air after an agonizingly long underwater swim. The good news was that I managed to steer clear of the trees below and right into a cornfield—which was actually a step up from a night jump I did in Arizona years earlier where I landed in a cactus *and* broke my nose. When my feet finally touched ground, I just laid there on my back for a good five minutes, with arms sprawled out to my sides as if I were making a snow angel, thinking to myself, *"Ho…ly…shit. Ho…ly…shit. Ho…ly…shit…"*

What did I learn from this? Not a damn thing, apparently, because I returned to the drop zone and immediately packed my chute to catch the next lift up.

However, this time I had some parachute riggers watch me pack just to mitigate any chance of operator error. Then, just before we boarded the caravan for takeoff, I partnered with a teammate nicknamed Badger because he was experienced, proficient, and as solid as any SEAL operator could aspire to be. I wanted him to watch my flying position for any tweaks, imbalances, or recommendations. When we landed, Badger gave me the "thumbs up" signal, which meant a lot coming from him, and we eventually boarded for a third jump.

Then it happened. Again.

The third jump that day was about as fun as the first. I went to pull the ripcord to deploy the canopy and instead of hearing the canopy deploy

I heard…crickets…crickets. Nothing. This time it was a bag lock—a full malfunction where only the bag in which the parachute is stuffed deploys from the container, but the chute itself stays packed—another less-than-desirable malfunction that you really can't fight your way out of. So, I initiated yet another cutaway procedure for the day. *Damnit, not again,* I thought to myself. I had performed more cutaways in that single day than some professional skydivers do in their entire careers—a little fun fact that I'm not very proud of. I don't remember where I landed but it certainly wasn't anywhere cool—more annoying than anything. Strangely, they weren't my last cutaways, either.

You might think that only a crazy person would live through multiple parachute malfunctions in one day and not quit on the spot. You're probably right. But something kept me coming back: it was my passion to stay with The Pack, and this wasn't the last time that my passion to stay with The Pack would be tested.

"The Pack" refers to a sense of belonging and unity that binds special operators together. It's a product of living, training, and fighting side by side; like the Spartans who used to carry a shield in the *Phalanx* less for their own protection than for that of the man next to them, it's a distinction that blurs the line between self and other, or between individual and team. But to be excluded from The Pack is to go through life with poor direction, little meaning, and a lack of fulfillment. When you have passion, you can easily answer "why." You wake up in the morning and go to work, and it's because the thought of answering your "why?" motivates you: because The Pack is there waiting for you.

Without direction, cause, zest, or "fire in the gut," the greater the opportunities open for regret, self-doubt, and despair—and they invade your mind because you begin to question what you do and why you do it. If you're passionate about your job, your relationships, and your hobbies, then the only thing that slows you down when challenge or hardship present themselves is the time it takes to reflect, learn, and move on. This answers the question of how, and why, you can keep jumping when your parachute keeps failing. When you are driven by passion and purpose, and guided by the emotional willingness to reflect, mental ability to learn, and spiritual capability of leaving it all behind to move on, you have all of the tools that you need to overcome adversity, and come out stronger on the other side

Purpose and passion go hand-in-hand no matter what role you're in, be it business, everyday life, or one's family. There can be no enthusiasm, no fervor, no meaning, and no happiness without answering the *why* of your pursuits.

How to "Steal" Passion

Passion and purpose have always been strong motivators for me right behind not getting shot—again. There must be an equal balance of the two to achieve optimal results, because a passion without purpose is akin to an untamed fire hose—it just sprays everything in its path with no direction, no guidance. Similarly, purpose without the passion to support it is the very feeling of creative tension we experience when we know what we want but take no action to "get there." It's this latter predicament that proves unsettling—to be in the driver's seat, map in hand, coffee mug full…and an empty tank of gas ("Where are you going? Nowhere!").

I contend that passion may be found by mirroring the artist. Think about it. Artists must be *truly* passionate about their work because it's all or nothing. They either love the painting they just created, or they tear up the canvas and start anew. There is constant refinement, never-ending improvement, and a perpetual desire to look for inspiration at every minute of the day. What a way to live, right?!

Leaders are no different. Leaders require both purpose and passion to inspire others because both are infectious, social contagions that spread like laughter or a bad case of herpes (yup, I said it).

Of course, being passionate is easier said than done, so let's look at what artists must do to achieve their desired optimal state—and how we can steal it:

1. **Passionate people work incessantly.** This is not to say that one's work life is more important than one's family life, but rather that the two coexist. In other words, there is no such thing as a work-life balance; you either enjoy what you do and whom you spend your time with, or you don't. You don't just "flip" the mental switch from one to another when you walk in the door.

2. **Passionate people create.** Artists take their imagination, turn it into an idea, create something tangible from it, and then put that creativity to use by innovating a new product. They are a one-stop supply-chain-shop who can take an idea and turn it into reality.

3. **Passionate people inspire others.** I don't know about you, but I've used "artsy" as an adjective to describe "those" types of people: those who are a little unique and willing to go against the social grain because they themselves are inspiring. People are inspired when

they see others doing something that they dream of doing—but choose not to.

4. **Passionate people are curious.** They seek answers. They want to know *why* things exist or why they occur, in order to improve them the next time.

5. **Passionate people find certainty.** Starting out at a blank canvas can be discomforting, but curiosity and a will to inspire drive passionate-bound people to create certainty where uncertainty exists. They're not afraid to take the first few steps into chaos and yell back to the rest of the crowd, "Hey, it's okay down here!"

6. **Passionate people don't ring the bell.** The challenge of becoming a Navy SEAL is almost a household conversation nowadays. In BUD/S (Basic Underwater Demolition/SEAL training), every Navy SEAL wannabe is a volunteer. If, at anytime, he (sorry gals) *doesn't* enjoy running around with a boat on his head, carrying a telephone pole with his team, or sitting in 55-degree Pacific Ocean water for days on end without sleep, he can just ring "the bell" three times and say, "I quit." Of the 174 students who started in my BUD/S class, only 34 of us (roughly 19 percent for all you "numbers" people) finished, because…

7. **Passionate people are driven to win.** They've identified—and envisioned—what *winning* looks like,

so all they need to do is fill in the gaps to get there. Artists don't give themselves any other options; they *must* produce if they want to continue being artists (and inspiring others, see #3).

8. **Passionate people adapt.** Much like the BUD/S student who adapts to the environment of SEAL training in order to pursue his purpose, passionate people are willing to fit the mold—any mold—if it means fueling his or her personal fire. They understand that it is possible to fit a square peg in a round hole by hammering it over and over until it fits, but they know the end state won't look pretty. Instead, passion drives creativity such that the artist realizes he can chip away at the preexisting peg until it's ready to fit.

9. **Passionate people believe in a "next state," not an "end state."** Failure is a mindset. It's a mindset of endless pursuit to improve because failure—unless it's death or taxes—is not an absolute state, only one's mindset to accept it is.

10. **Passionate people practice constantly.** Nothing good ever comes overnight, and anything worth doing is worth doing correctly. I remember a saying one of our SEAL instructors used to say—in-between curse words and other pithy comments that I can't repeat here—which was, "There are two ways to do

something: Right, and again." Artists don't settle for a mediocre expression of themselves. Instead, they hone their skills of focus, concentration, authenticity, and self-expression every day—something inherent in effective leaders.

11. **Passionate people keep their work.** An artist's past work serves as a source of reflection (and inspiration) to measure past lessons learned and overall improvement. Much like the after-action review (post mortem) in the military where the intent is to examine any discrepancies between intended purpose and actual outcome, an artist compares his or her work to the source that defines "success," where *success* in this case means matching product to purpose.

12. **Passionate people perform.** Performance—superior performance—doesn't come by itself, but rather from consistency of practice and a willingness to learn. What enables learning is the desire (read: passion) to throw ego to the wayside in light of the higher purpose: to improve.

Just as effective leaders practice the fundamentals of leadership daily (i.e. honesty, openness, integrity, courage), passionate people practice the "artist's way" of passionate living daily—and performance is the result. Truly, nobody yields optimal results without at least a hint of passion.

Love of the Game: The Pitfalls of Too Much Passion

Of course, too much of one thing can be just that—too much. As mentioned previously, purpose and passion unharnessed can turn into a violent, untamed fire hose that devastates everything in its path. Too much passion can have the detrimental effect of indecision, as an over-affinity induces an emotional dependence that is hard to pull away from. An overabundance of passion inhibits adaptability.

Love of the game is an insidious threat because it opens the floodgates of opportunity and plays to the fire burning in your gut. Your desire to fuel it becomes so overpowering that you don't stop to evaluate it, but rather *Go! Go! Go!* and therefore skip details in the process because you're moving so fast. These details begin as minor fissures, but later, they turn into major cracks in the foundation. Consider, for a moment, a carpenter. He or she must be *spot on* when it comes to measurement, because being off even an eighth of an inch at the beginning of a cut will turn into a huge, one-inch gap later on. Similarly, if you keep running in the same direction but choose not to slow down to review and refine your mission, then you're just running toward the wrong place faster.

I saw this firsthand as an organizational adaptability consultant at the McChrystal Group. I was part of a client team assigned to a remarkably fast-growing apparel and performance company whose challenge was not a bad to challenge to have, but challenging nonetheless. This company, because of their explosive growth, didn't take the time to reflect and renew their processes and past performance. They were so forward-looking that their passion to win and continue growing superseded their willingness to learn and reflect.

Lessons Learned

Passion can be a two-headed snake with a yin-yang effect, and the only determination you have to make is which voice (yin or yang) you listen to. It's easy to listen to the voice of simplicity, the one that's pushing for immediate feedback *now* because, well, who doesn't like gratitude? However, the more you cede to the simple things in life, the harder life becomes. Take exercise, for example. There are two choices when it comes to starting an exercise routine: do it or don't do it. The simple choice is obviously not to do it, but choosing that path only creates greater frustration, lack of fulfillment, and unhappiness down the road—all physical, mental, and emotional impediments to performance. Life gets harder.

However, choosing the difficult decisions in life tends to make living *easier*. Continuing with the exercise example, there are myriad studies about how adhering to a routine fitness regimen enhances mental acuity, lowers one's predisposition to illness and disease, and improves overall physical health. Life gets easier.

Passion and purpose are critical to performance. My passion to become a SEAL was at a constant level twelve in college (on a scale of one to ten with ten being die-hard enthusiasm). I exercised five days a week back then—running, swimming, and performing calisthenics—to keep my mind and body's "finger on the pulse" of being ready for BUD/S. I used to set personal challenges for myself to build mental toughness, like waking up at five in the morning to go to the gym—rain, sleet, or snow—even if I had only one class scheduled that day and it wasn't until noon. I was so adamant about exercising and building up my physical and mental stamina that I got to the point where I would have three midterm exams in a day with an hour and a half break in-between. So, instead of stressing out over the next exam like most students, I would go for a run-swim-run (three mile run, one mile swim, three mile run), and *then* go take the exam because I thought this would test my mental capacity to "shift gears;" to switch from a physical "high peak" to a mental "high peak." I considered every exam an opportunity to test my mental prowess (or lack thereof). Rather than conceding to the uncertainty of fear and failure, exams became personal challenges and opportunities for me to excel—a way to manage my perspective and take the "temperature" of my academic competence.

The self-imposed stress that students (and people, for that matter) place on themselves is just that—self-imposed—and it is a direct result of *how* they see a particular problem. All it takes is a little shift in perspective to reveal a new vantage point over your enemy—whatever that "enemy" may be—that is compelling enough to create and sustain a new way to focus on the problem.

Stress, anxiety, apprehension are all choices we make in response to how we *choose* to see an issue or behavior. Stephen Covey, in his bestseller *The 7 Habits of Highly Effective People,* showed that in-between *stimulus* and *response* there is a gap, and it is within that gap where *choice* resides. How we interpret daily activities and interactions—more than the activity or interaction itself—is what defines reality, not the activities themselves. We can either choose to see a test as a potential for failure, or as an opportunity to improve—as a way to demonstrate how well your studies and diligent efforts have paid off. Achieving any feat depends on how you see and define *success* relative to your position, and how much effort you're willing to expend in order to overcome the chaos in-between.

If there's one thing that I've done right in my life, it has been to face head-on that which I fear the most. Nobody likes living with regrets, which is why facing reality when the opportunity presents itself is so important. If you really think about it, there are two sources of fear in the human mind, and each one resides on opposite ends of the spectrum. There is *uncertainty*, and there is *certainty*. The intermediary space in-between these two elements is the gray area where strength and weakness coexist. Attributes like courage, anxiety, consequence, and purpose all reside in-between these mental North and South poles and are just waiting to spring into action once you choose the right one for the job. No element within this gray area knows what direction to head until you define the problem and choose your response. By filling this space with justification that supports your focus, you move more toward certainty, character, and competence, and away from the emotional toxins of anxiety and trepidation that hinder personal growth. Remember, fear conquers fear.

In college, I used to think that in order to be really productive, I needed to apply every waking moment of the day toward studying because that was the only way to internalize the classroom material. Cramming at the last minute didn't make sense to me because, at the end of four years, what good were my efforts if I couldn't remember anything? So, I jam packed my days with study time, flashcards, review, and reading. Even worse, I began to feel guilty when I *wasn't* doing something to better myself. I used to think, "Why am I wasting *valuable time* resting? I need to work!" What happened was, I became a victim of my own passion.

There were three flaws with this belief. First, everybody needs rest. Rest (and reflection) is the only time that you actually grow, internalize the day's processes and lessons learned, and innovate new solutions to old problems. It's what enables growth. Muscle is not built *during* exercise, but rather during the rest periods in-between and overnight—the brain is just another muscle (metaphorically speaking). Secondly, I realized that it was *my perspective* that was self-defeating, not the "valuable time" I needed to dedicate toward studying. And third, the idea that I would actually remember anything from college was just ignorant in itself (that's a joke).

My sophomore year in college my sister and I lived together. She was—and is—awesome, and we are still close friends. However, after that year in college she moved to California and so my roommate, sibling, and close friend disappeared, only to be seen yearly thereafter. The perspective on how I defined "valuable time" changed, as I wished that I had not been so focused on academic performance. If you think about it, to focus on some*thing* is to exclude everything else. Being single-minded on one *thing* can debilitate growth and personal reward from other areas. Too much passion can be too much.

The fact is, how you see and define success, productivity, and personal time can all be changed at any point. All it takes is a mental gearshift to refocus and assign a new value to your purpose to reignite that passion. The trick, however, is the learning, unlearning, and relearning processes that go with it that fuel your skillset, and that's what the next chapter is about.

The 5C's of Chaos

"You gotta be fucking kidding me."

The danger is greatest when the finish line is in sight.

—Steven Pressfield

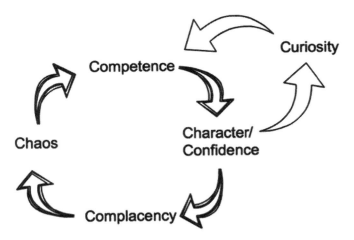

T o become a SEAL, you must want to become exceptional and pursue that desire relentlessly. It doesn't happen overnight. Rather, it's a constant process of learning—not just through countless training evolutions and scenarios, but also through self-awareness and self-evaluation. Throughout my own personal learning process, I've observed a pattern emerge within my experience that I'd like to share with you—I call it the 5Cs.

The 5Cs refers to the cycle by which competence can actually lead to chaos. It sounds impossible—shouldn't increasing your competence and skill set be a decent buffer against encroaching chaos? Sure, in some scenarios—you can't clear a house safely, win the Super Bowl, or even teach a child to read without some competence in whatever you're trying to achieve. But competence has a dark side, too, one that I've seen time and again in my own experience. It can lead to complacency, and when the stakes are life and death, complacency kills.

How do the 5Cs work? Let's first look at this through the optic of shooting. While I had some experience with firearms before entering SEAL training, it was in the Teams that I developed the level of proficiency in shooting that enabled me to eventually rise to the highest level of the SEAL Teams. I learned to shoot the way that anyone learns any new skill: patiently and methodically, slowly becoming a better shot through repetition, perpetual learning, and application. As competence grew, so too did confidence—and with increased confidence came increased risk (and responsibility).

There is nothing as dangerous as becoming overconfident, whether it be on the shooting range or elsewhere. If your competence and confidence are so high that you're no longer challenged, then what happens? Complacency sets in. You begin taking safety for granted. You start taking riskier shots that challenge *you* but place other peoples' lives at stake. Then it happens. Chaos arrives and you either shoot yourself or, even worse, somebody else. When that happens, back to the drawing board of competence you go. And the cycle continues.

Generally speaking, the pattern is this: greater competence leads to more confidence; confidence builds character; and from there, you come to a crossroads. You have to choose for yourself what comes next; is it going to be complacency, or curiosity? Two different paths, and one—complacency—leads to chaos, while the other—curiosity—empowers you to steer clear of disaster and refresh the cycle of learning. Curiosity keeps you on your toes and keeps you humble—both of which are the antitheses of complacency.

But what happens if you take the wrong road, and, lacking self-awareness, you slip from confidence into *over*confidence? You know it all, you've seen it all, you've got nothing left to learn. Overconfidence is a dangerous place because that's when complacency sets in—and remember, complacency kills.

Northern Afghanistan, February 2010

"Delta rasha, delta rasha!" I yelled, the Pashto command for "come here." *This chick isn't listening. Where the hell is this guy?* I thought to myself. We were targeting a high level Taliban commander and I was point man along a corner wall with the assault force behind. The lady facing me was holding a baby in her arms and standing under an archway with an open door on either side of her.

"Delta rasha!" I yelled again, and then commanded her to turn around so I could see if there were any bulges protruding out from her dress, which would be indicators of weapons or explosives. She refused to obey. *What the fuck!?* I was getting mad. *Does she* want *to get shot?* I quietly asked myself.

◆◆◆

Just a few months prior, we had told some inhabitants to come out of their building, and as they did, there was a male wearing a dress and a head wrap while carrying—yet another—baby. He embedded himself with the other females of the house in an attempt to pass himself off as a woman and avoid detection. We wanted to separate the women and kids from the men—something the enemy already knew—which was why this insurgent was posing as a woman.

But something wasn't right. In the moonlight, the faces of all the women were clearly identifiable through our night vision goggles, and one face was different from the rest—"her" face was dirty. As the group moved closer to us, the shadow on "her" face remained still. The shadow, as it turned out, was a beard. *That's a…dude,* I thought. "That's a fucking dude!" I passed over the radio. I wasn't about to let this guy get any closer.

Just two deployments prior to this one, a suicide bomber had created a whole new set of context for me to base my decisions and rules of engagement on (see "Strategizing Chaos"). However, instead of shooting this time, I chose to exercise a bit of tactical patience, because I just didn't see the need to shoot yet. Tactical patience refers to an operator's impulse control; it is his ability to see myriad possibilities into which a situation can unravel, but he remains cool, calm, and collected so as not get lost in the web of complexity. He is always ready—physically, mentally, and emotionally—to face whatever challenges are forthcoming, but he doesn't "jump the gun" and make any assumptions. Conflict is inevitable, and he knows it. (More on this later.)

So I told the group of women to stop and lift their veils. They refused because Afghan culture restricts women from showing their faces in public or to other males. Of course, guns can have a way of causing people to second-guess their faith. Moreover, war is no place for cultural sensitivities. We (the United States) tend to shoot ourselves in the foot over this concept;

we believe that having higher morals on the battlefield is indicative of superiority, but it isn't. It leads to hesitancy, second-guessing, and unclear rules of engagement. Unfortunately, the ones who dictate policy are never the same ones who pull the trigger. It's a leadership gap.

Truthfully, adhering to local customs wasn't really at the forefront of my mind at this particular moment in time, so I motioned for all the women to lift their veils, and they all did so, except one—the "woman" with the bearded face refused.

Meanwhile, the other women were beginning to piece together what was happening, and they slowly began backing away from him. He was still holding the baby, so I ordered him to put the baby down. The last thing we needed was a baby with a broken neck. After one last-ditch effort for this guy to put the baby down, he finally agreed. He then placed his hands where I couldn't see them. That was all the permission I needed.

There's an element of patience and judgment here that's worth highlighting. Taking that shot while he was holding the baby would've been easy, but it could've produced more harm than good because the baby would've been hurt—not injured, but hurt. It's a fine line to mentally navigate—the situational awareness, the enemy's hand motions and facial expressions—especially in a fraction of a second in the face of uncertainty.

I was not about to run the risk of him clacking himself off, so I expelled a few rounds from my rifle (followed by the typical hailstorm of bullets from the rest of the team) and dropped the cross-dressing insurgent right there. A funny thing in the Teams is that when one guy initiates a shot, *everybody* follows suit, almost as if there is just last one dessert on the dinner table and everybody wants a piece. As it turned out, this insurgent had an anti-personnel mine on him that he probably wasn't planning on turning over.

♦♦♦

So, fast forward back to where we are now—in a compound targeting yet another al-Qaeda leader, and facing yet another "lady" holding a baby, crying, and refusing our commands. More kids trickled out and swarmed her like pups fighting for their mom's tit. She refused to exit the doorway or obey any of my commands, as she must have thought she was immune to bullets. Unfortunately, we had in the past had no choice but to kill women who posed direct threats to us, but this one wasn't exactly a danger to us; just noncompliant. Of course, a threat is a threat is a threat. It's an ugly truth but the fact of the matter is that there is no prejudice in war, and when you need to kill an idea for national security, you need to kill everyone with it.

She refused our command to turn around once more, and in the next instant she made one swift move and darted across the doorway into another room to the right, leaving the archway unobstructed. Unfortunately for me, however, she was in the reactionary gap, which is the distance between you and an opponent that yields to the first move every time. The farther you are outside of that gap (i.e. the farther away you are from the stimulus), the easier it is to react, because you have more time. Think of a football quarterback. If the best quarterback in the NFL were to throw his hardest, fastest pass to you with your hands down at a distance of about eight yards, you probably would not have time to react. But, if you increase that distance to fifty yards, you can now see the pass coming much more easily—and you have more time to react because you are now *outside* the reactionary gap. No matter how much you train your reflexes, no matter how fast you can pull the trigger, if you are being acted upon while "in the gap," then you are already a step behind. Action will beat reaction to the punch—or trigger—every time.

I received the squeeze from the guy behind me, thought to myself, *Here we go,* and took three purposeful yet methodical steps, only to be met by…

Bap! Bap! Bap! Bap! Bap! Bap! An insurgent with an AK stepped out from underneath the awning right into the reactionary gap and let out a short burst from his rifle before any of us could react. He came out after his wife and kids had moved across the archway to cover, as if he was the last item being tugged on a rope, and began spraying from the hip just like that other insurgent in Iraq three years prior.

The first machine gun burst caught me three times—once in the forearm, once in the shoulder, and once dead center in my chest plate. Body armor once again saved my life, but unlike the first time I was shot, these rounds hurt—a lot.

Are you fucking kidding me?! was the first thing that came to mind. I was so pissed off, not just for getting shot but for getting shot *again.* I scurried out of the way, so the assaulters behind me could pick up my slack and hose this dude.

Meanwhile, two other team members who had been next to me fell back. *They must have been hit, too*, I thought to myself. *Damn.* The three of us scrambled out of the way to allow for the rest of the team to get in there and finish this guy.

As I sat outside trying to help my buddy get his medical pack out with my other hand, I began to feel faint. Later, I realized I was just being a baby because I wasn't really bleeding severely anywhere. But I had to sit down and have someone check out my injuries. In that minute of shock and haze, I began to ask myself, *Is this it? Am I going to die here? Right now?* I thought about my then-wife and how sad she was going to be. I thought about what an *asshole* I had been recently, and how sorry I was, and that I may not ever get the opportunity to say, "I'm sorry." I thought about all my friends who had passed away within recent years, how the command memorializes them by hanging their pictures on the wall, and how my picture was going to be up next.

I continued feeling sorry for myself while the team members checked out my injuries until another voice entered my head, stronger and more rational than the first one—and far more appealing. This new voice offered no sympathy; it just said, simply, *"I'm not fucking dying here."* And that was it. That tiny declaration was all I needed to realize that my story was not about to end on top of a pile of crap in Northern Afghanistan. The same voice that suggested to model the way after being hit the first time, to find a way to *not lose*, told me something else that night. It said, "Get the fuck up."

My mind was made up, and I was going to quit being a sissy and walk off the damn battlefield. After all, I was only shot through the forearm and the shoulder. I looked at the guy next to me, who I'll call Lucifer, as he was hit, too, but his injury was much more serious than mine. The bullet blazed a trail about half an inch left of his heart. I began to worry about losing yet another brother. And then I saw my other buddy, who I'll again call J, had been shot through the hip. *Damn.*

Both team members suffered injuries, but in the end, both fully recovered. An interesting little fun fact was that the same shooting buddy who I was next to in Iraq the first time I was shot—J—was next to me this time. Funny how things come full circle.

While the three of us were medevac'd out, the assault force dealt with a pretty decent barricaded shooter in the compound. Here's what happened afterward.

The insurgent had run back into his dwelling where he barricaded himself. The team tried an alternate entry point that happened to be right on top of the insurgent, and by "on top" I mean *on top*. They set an explosive breach, blew the door in, and the door was so heavy that it didn't explode but rather just fell, and it fell on top of the insurgent. The assault force made entry but didn't see him in the room, until about two seconds later when the insurgent apparently had reached out from underneath the door, fired aimlessly into the darkness, and the muzzle flash of his rifle singed the beard of one of the team members in the room. One member was standing right above the insurgent who lay on the ground underneath the door.

This insurgent had a purpose. He had a passion to kill Americans and to keep killing Americans, and it drove him to fight to his death. How do you defend against that? This was a battle that we all faced because bullets and brawn is no match for personal ideals. Sure, you may get them to *say* whatever you want, but you're not going to get them to *believe* it.

Now, this had been my sixth deployment (out of eight total). I had been shot three deployments earlier in Iraq and I believe I felt a bit of confidence knowing the fact that I had already "checked" that box; in thinking that since I got shot once, that it wouldn't likely happen again. Boy was I wrong.

The only way to mitigate the pitfalls of complacency or catastrophe is to remain humble and realize that who you were yesterday has no impact upon who you are today (more on humility in "Filling the Knowledge Gap"). The SEAL motto of "the only easy day was yesterday," a saying that was instilled in us during BUD/S, served as a reminder to remain forever humble and always vigilant, because the second you let your guard down is when the enemy of catastrophe strikes.

Vigilance is a perpetual mindset. To be vigilant is to be open to possibility, because you see a bigger picture and are able to connect the dots between people, events, and relationships, while always considering the potential for change to arise. Being mindful of areas for development helps keep you humbly focused on your purpose *because* you're aware that anything can happen at any moment.

Competence alone does not yield success. It may bring confidence, but not the other way around. Complacency appears when one's competence goes unchallenged; when one is overly poised to act. In the resulting chaos, catastrophe ensues.

Now, while getting shot so often certainly wasn't fun, it paled in comparison to losing teammates. There was a stretch of time where we lost a teammate almost every month, which served as a reminder that nobody is invincible. Ultimately, when complacency did set in for me, I knew it was time to move on. I was burned out. The situations we faced were no longer challenging. We had been exposed to stressors, risks, and uncertainties that would make most people cry. We solved the impossible, and we did it routinely. Everything—*everything*—becomes boring if you do it enough, and chasing bad guys was no different. My attitude reflected it, as did my beliefs, intentions, and expectations. This, in turn, determined the choices that determined my behavior—which ultimately led to chaos.

The First "C" of Chaos: Competence

If you look at what great teams do and how they succeed, it all boils down to how an *ordinary* group of individuals works together in an *extra*ordinary manner toward a shared objective or purpose. Success is a factor of *who* they are (character), *what* they can do (competence), and *how* they communicate. Honesty, enthusiasm, and a positive attitude are all useless without the capacity for action, but action becomes futile when 5C's of Chaos interfere.

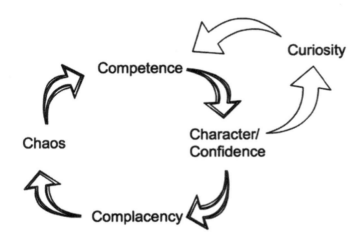

What the above figure reflects is this: the central four "C's"—competence, character and confidence, complacency, chaos—all exist along a spectrum of cause/effect. Here's how.

The more Joe, for example, performs his job the more competent he becomes. His character grows as he becomes more confident. As time goes on, however, Joe feels less and less challenged, because his job has become routine and his skills have grown marginally at best. He has a greater overall awareness than when he started, but over time he has slipped into complacency. Joe no longer scrutinizes every email. He no longer attends meetings with the same rigor and appetite for learning that he once did. He doesn't feel the need to read everything that comes across his desk because, well, he has already been at the company for six years. Joe's complacency has now become a placeholder for chaos to ensue. However, there's a way around this potential for disaster, and that is to stay hungry; to remain curious by continually asking why and perpetually learning and seeking improvement.

9/11: Complacency

The US had an opportunity to kill/capture Osama bin Laden in the late 1990s, but chose not to. Why? My contention is that we were complacent. We were competent as a world superpower, confident that we would remain so, and probably even a little complacent since no "major" attacks on the homeland had occurred.

Then, on September 11th, everything changed.

Catastrophe struck because complacency had set in throughout the government. *Everyone* was at fault, not a single agency or leader. What's even worse is the fact that people became complacent just *after* 9/11. It is easy for some people to forget quickly, and unfortunately it takes a disaster to remind them.

Operation Urgent Fury, 1983: (In)Competence

The invasion of Grenada was the first major operation conducted by the US military since the Vietnam War—and everybody wanted a part in it. Nearly eight thousand soldiers, airmen, marines, and sailors participated in the event, with the majority of them being special operators. From the SEAL perspective, we had three missions:

1. To rescue and evacuate the governor from his mansion

2. Secure a radio tower

3. Emplace homing beacons on the Salinas airstrip in support of a future Ranger assault

The team of SEALs and Air Force combat controllers (CCTs) who were supposed to position the beacons planned to parachute into the water, link up with their zodiac boats, then rendezvous at a point just offshore and swim into the beach. Unfortunately, the knee-jerk reaction of senior leaders in Washington and the apparent urgency of the situation led to a culmination of late intel developments, poor decision-making, and slight degrees of incompetence—all of which resulted in four SEALs drowning at sea.

Complacency was not the issue. Overconfidence was not the issue. The problem was the incompetence that arose out of senior decision makers' intent for self-promotion (organizationally speaking). You see, each branch of service wanted to prove its worth, and some of the decisions made tended to supersede the likelihood of success. Chaos ensued.

Operation Gothic Serpent, 1993

US Army Rangers had conducted routine missions throughout the city of Mogadishu, Somalia, in support of their mission to capture terrorist leaders led by local warlord Mohamed Farrah Aidid. With zero casualties as a testament of their skill, the task force's confidence and competence were both high; nothing "significant" had happened thus far in their mission. Some would say that this created a bit of complacency—and this is when disaster struck, turning something routine into something chaotic. Because of this, the story of the battle of Mogadishu is etched into history as an unfortunate lesson in urban warfare, a day in which seventeen brave servicemen would be killed in action and a horrific scenario would take place that still plagues Washington's decision-making to this day, now known as Black Hawk Down.

What all three of these examples illustrate is that you can enter this cycle at any point. In the cases of 9/11 and the battle of Mogadishu, different types of complacency led to chaos, while the outcome of Operation Urgent Fury demonstrates that a confluence of factors both within and outside of our control might come into play (ego, confusion, and good old-fashioned "shit hitting the fan"). Ultimately, though, the outcome is always the same: chaos will always result—unless the cycle is interrupted.

Breaking the Cycle of Chaos: Competence and Curiosity

A goal without a plan is just a dream, feedback without personal reflection is merely criticism, and behavior without a purpose is a mistake. Anywhere you look, execution requires the physical, mental, emotional, and spiritual competencies to merge the dividing line between thinking and doing. The trick, of course, is to learn how.

The greater one's level of competence, the closer one moves to becoming *extra*ordinary. So, to define what *extra*ordinary is, it may be valuable to first examine what *ordinary* looks like in today's business environment:

- *No meeting agendas*

- *Nonexistent or poorly articulated roles, responsibilities, and expectations*

- *Poor communication between people, departments*

- *No alignment and therefore no accountability*

- *Different missions across different departments (the sales division has a different goal than the marketing department)*

- *Lack of trust between people and departments*

- *Leaders not leading—that is, leaders who are risk-averse, don't understand their team's capabilities, avoid accountability, or make egocentric decisions*

- *People serving themselves rather than serving others*

- *Little focus on personal development or leadership succession*

- *No purpose, and therefore little energy to work*

- *Unwillingness to adapt to change or new demands*

Is this normal for you? Your organization? Why? How much trust would you, the head of your sales division, for instance, put in someone in marketing to make a decision for you? Probably zero because you each have different purposes, different knowledge bases, and different conceptions of what *right* looks like. Moreover, the lack of trust exists because there are no forums to share knowledge, strategize, or build trust. More on this later.

Just as there is chaos that exists at the individual level, competence is an organizational necessity, too. How we—in the Teams—answered the need for improvement—and hence, bred more competence—was through information sharing.

Building Organizational Competence: Cross-Pollination

In the Naval Special Warfare community, the extensive capabilities of the Teams opened the door for more and more operational considerations by senior political leaders and, therefore, more chances for us to test our competencies against the unknown.

Cross-pollination was a process we performed in the Teams to spread the wealth of knowledge and experience from one team to another. If you really think about it, individual competence is certainly important for any organization because it contributes to overall performance. But individual performance alone is inconsequential. Here's why. Progress— within any team or company—is a function of relationships; the process of how individuals work together or successively toward a shared objective determines results.

Cross-pollination bred this. Prior to cross-pollinizing, each team had its own "personality," and standard operating procedures (SOPs), and the SOPs from one squadron would, historically, stay with just *that* particular squadron. SOPs ranged from the tactical to the operational (i.e. from daily execution to logistics and execution). But by interjecting an apple with an orange, so to speak, members began to develop the taste for a new food—or tactic, in our case. While nobody really looked forward to changing teams after having invested so much time with the guys they had lived, trained, traveled, and fought with, cross-pollinating was an indispensable tool not just for personal improvement, but for enhancing our own competencies, as well. The intra-exchange led to greater shared learning across the community and bridged any communicative gaps that pervaded the command since each member had his own informal network of operators with whom he would confide and share information. Thus, the lessons learned from training and real world missions spread like a wildfire throughout the command, because there were well-placed "nodes" in each and every network.

The repercussions of not cross-pollinating were similar to the issues I've seen in companies today:

- *Haphazard decision-making based on limited information*

- *Lack of trust due to poor communication*

- *Redundant work efforts that cost the company time and money*

In SEAL terms, Joe—our favorite fictional character—has been raised as an assaulter in one team his whole career. His myopic experience makes him a subject matter expert when it comes to planning raids and conducting assaults, but less adept when new missions arise. He's less competent in other mission sets where an assault isn't feasible. He soon learns that as fun as it is to be a hammer, not everything needs a pounding. If you are a bull and the target is a china shop, then the risk to force you *not* to break anything is too great, which means you and your know-how are now obsolete.

Certain skills may be in-demand at one time, but what happens tomorrow or next year when the enemies, operating environments, and trends all change? Just as in hockey, basketball, football, or any other sport, you want to set yourself up for success and go to where the puck or ball will be, not to where it is. By staying in a single skill set your whole career, you become limited by what you know and handicapped by what you don't. You lack the diversified know-how that others have of putting students through training to understand *why* trainees do stupid things, of grasping the systemic layout of curriculum design from beginning to end, for example. Hence, your focus and your contribution stay myopic at best. You operate in a silo.

Such a narrow view can be an intellectual setback that creates tunnel vision and impedes learning which was why, at my last command, there was a mandatory professional development rotation instituted after spending four years in a team. Much to guys' chagrin—including myself, at the time—it actually produced more-experienced operators. Team members could better understand how each organizational piece fit together and why, which allowed them to better understand the whole puzzle. This practice of professional diversity also helped shape the mindset of each member because they learned how to assimilate themselves into new situations, new environments, and develop the soft skills that were lacking from years of shooting bad guys in the face. Wearing a suit and tie in an embassy requires a very different skillset than throwing on fatigues and heading onto the battlefield.

Cross-pollination was effective, as members were soon deployed overseas outside their comfort zones. This increase in knowledge sharing and experience enabled us to influence key decision makers and communicate our purpose in a language that everyone understood, rather than what we—SEALs—had all previously relied upon: shooting a tight "group" or wearing cool-guy sunglasses (which we still do, by the way). Nobody believes what you can do until they understand the type of person you are. Despite the fact that nobody wanted to leave the team for a professional development tour, each member returned with greater awareness that only led to sustained superior performance.

Consider the repercussions of silo-ing yourself into one single capability. What if an unfortunate casualty occurs and you are asked to support or fill in a new role but you have no idea what the responsibilities, standards, or competencies entail? This actually happens more often than not in many organizations. Consider the following hypothetical (but all too often, very true) situation of a fictional marketing director named Matt who just received a promotion to vice president. Matt has been promoted according to the competence he displayed from the time he entered the organization up through every promotion opportunity. This metric for advancement lasted roughly up to his new role as vice president of marketing. Once in the C-suite, his ability to deliver and execute (i.e. competence) is no longer the metric for success but rather the expectation.

Instead, Matt is now measured on his character and how well he *navigates* relationships to work and achieve results collaboratively. Matt's success now depends less on functional expertise and more on general knowledge. However, he never received the "memo" on how to bridge this promotion gap, what leadership looks like, and how it would differ from his role as a director.

Even worse, Matt wasn't even aware that such a gap existed in the first place. Now, he must stay current with not only the tangible skills of his job function (the expectation) but also learn the intangibles such as presence, communication, and leadership associated with his newfound promotion.

The key to success in the above scenario is to recognize that different competencies exist at different levels, and anticipating what those competencies are affords the very opportunity to smack chaos in the face when it emerges and say, "Fuck you, not today."

DACA: Detect, Adapt, Choose, Adopt

Here is a four-step process I call DACA for how to change your leadership style and adapt to the right situation:

Step 1: Detect. The first step to any sort of change is to identify the imperative to change. In the military, before we set out to plan our next mission we first needed to understand the environment in which we operated. Specifically, we needed to discern between two types of unknowns. The first is known unknowns, such as our capabilities, enemy pattern of life, and likely or unlikely responses. The second type is unknown unknowns, and these are indicated by the weather, terrain, and—again—enemy behavior. The degree to which we could anticipate an enemy's response dictated our approach, much like understanding the relationship dynamics, interests, and vested resources amongst stakeholders in a meeting.

The point is, don't be that guy or gal to enter into a new situation assuming you know everything, because once you do, there's no turning back. First impressions are lasting impressions. Instead, you want to calibrate the most effective way to deliver results, so take the time to let every situation unravel to better understand the situational dynamics.

Step 2: Adapt. The reason detection is so important is because it affords *space* to maneuver—not in the physical sense of trying to escape another seemingly wasteful meeting, but the *mental space* that allows you to adjust mid-course based on new information or perspectives—and this is where adaptability comes in.

To adapt in this sense is to have a flexible mindset; to be prepared to put aside the functional expertise and instead improvise based on the intent of the situation and the best fit for its purpose. Of course, a flexible mindset is easier said than done. We all know people who are anything but flexible in their ways.

Step 3: Choose. Choosing the right leadership style depends on a number of factors. Here are a few questions to consider before choosing the best leadership style to employ:

- *What does "right" look like? Is my definition of winning the same as everybody else's?*

- *What objective am I trying to achieve? What objective are we trying to achieve? Why the discrepancy? (if applicable)*

- *What and who will be impacted the most? Is this impact in accordance with our intent?*

Step 4: Adopt. Once you've detected the right leadership style to employ, adapted your mindset and behavior to that style, and effectively chosen to implement it into practice, it's time to actually do it. Adopting a new leadership style into your repertoire allows you to call upon that style and its associated skills at any time and under any circumstance.

The DACA approach can help you slow down your thought process and settle into the situation before diving in too deep. Take the time to let the situation unravel and then apply the right leadership style to the right situation.

When an employee is raised in one particular light, he or she can't help but see one way to solve problems because that's all he or she knows. It can prove to be fatal, as the next vignette will show.

Khowst, Afghanistan 2009

A note to readers: What follows is the story of an individual whose incompetence had life or death repercussions for herself and seven other Americans whose lives depended on her leadership. My objective here is not to speak ill of the dead, but to illustrate the point

*that, in a combat zone where there is no room for failure and chaos
is knocking at the door, competence is everything.*

In 2009, I was part of a small team dedicated to an outpost in
Southeastern Afghanistan. Our mission was to gather intelligence and
generate target packages in collaboration with other governmental
agencies (OGA) and the DOD. The key piece to this relationship was the
"collaboration" part, since there were only two SEALs (myself and another)
assigned to this outfit, so we needed the OGA's participation as well as host
nation forces to help prosecute targets.

However, our counterpart, who I'll call Lisa, was the chief of base and
saw things differently. As the chief of base, Lisa's primary responsibility
was the safety and security of every man and woman on that base. Her
secondary responsibility was to develop human intelligence (humint)
among the local populace and share that intel with us so that we—OGA
and DOD—could work together and put the smackdown on bad guys. Just
to add more fuel to the fire, we (SEALs) were a two-man team supported
by three to four other personnel who were not operational, which meant
that we *needed* to play nicely with others since they had all the manpower.
However, we had military assets that they did not, so the need for each
other was mutual, depending on the mission.

Lisa believed that the DOD had no experience in human intelligence
collection and that we should leave the intel and source meetings to the
"professionals" (i.e. them). As a result, Lisa refused to share their weekly
and daily plans with us, which only hindered progress.

Instead, another SEAL (who I'll call J) and I pressed on with trying
to open communication channels with Lisa for the simple fact that, if
we didn't communicate, we were dead in the water operationally. J and
I came from an organization where meetings actually served a purpose,

because there was an agenda and there was accountability for decisions. An established meeting agenda allows you to be proactive instead of reactive, because it offers answers, direction, and guidance (more on this in "An Adaptive Environment").

So, we proposed to Lisa that our two groups do an initial meet and greet and from there establish a routine for face-to-face get-togethers— nothing formal, just a brief ten minutes to say "these are our intentions, these are our resources, and these are our resultant priorities." She was on board, but reluctant.

We had our precious little meeting during which *we* shared things openly and transparently. After all, we were there to work together and take the fight to al Qaeda, not against each other. At least, that was our perspective.

Lisa shared some information with us, but it was her unwillingness to trust that eventually led to her demise. Unbeknownst to us, she had a "high level source" that claimed access to number al Qaeda's number two—Ayman al-Zawahiri, Osama bin Laden's deputy. One day, Lisa's source decided he was going to come in to base and reveal everything he knew to his handlers. The day the source was brought onto base, there was no physical search of him and he was treated as as close to a VIP as possible. As the chief of base it was Lisa's duty to ensure the safety of the men and women there, which was her first failure. The man was brought to a secure location about thirty yards behind our building. Once collected, the man was told to wait for more "important" people to arrive because they wanted to be a part of whatever he had to say, so the Jordanian agreed to wait. Finally, all the participants arrived and gathered in a circle around the informant. Meanwhile, another OGA analyst was walking over to the meeting room carrying a birthday cake for their beloved asset.

KA-BOOOOM!

All of a sudden, the building erupted in a tremendous explosion. It knocked the birthday-toting analyst flat on her back. Carnage of American bodies littered the grounds. The "source" was an al Qaeda double agent, who used Lisa's inexperience and arrogance to kill her and eight others, not to mention create the single most devastating event in the history of the CIA.

Our sole purpose on that base was to provide tactical context. When it came to tactics and mission planning, we were the experts—not OGA. Any time a foreign national comes onto a base, he or she gets searched. It's a very simple protocol and takes less than a minute.

Fortunately, J and I had left the outpost about a week prior to this tragic event. My heart goes out to the families of the men and women who served under Lisa, because she was way above her head and had no business playing the role she did. She had done other tours prior to this post in Afghanistan where the only bad guys sat on bar stools. The main reason she was on that base was to get the overseas "check in the box" that diversified her experience (at least on paper) and would propel her to the next level. Ego kills.

Lisa failed for multiple reasons, four of which are significant enough to discuss here. The first failure was already mentioned—complete disregard for security protocol. The second was her organizational upbringing. Through no fault of her own, Lisa was raised in a silo that created a biased viewpoint and consequently taught her to look one way at a problem. When she moved up in rank, a gap was created between what she knew previously and what was asked of her. In other words, what got Lisa her promotion was different from what would cause her to excel.

I believe that cross-pollination throughout Lisa's career path would have served as a much broader optic through which to see the war. Lisa would have had more mental tools and experiences to pull from that could have shaped her judgment. In turn, the limited experience she had was what created a poor ability to trust and communicate with others.

The third failure was ego. Arrogance can severely degrade one's self-efficacy—the ability produce results; to *perform*—if improperly managed, as it prevents oneself from seeing the bigger picture—any picture—and therefore precludes learning from others. Overconfident and arrogant individuals see one thing as central to all decision-making: themselves. Lisa made the decision to forego a security search of the source because she feared insulting him and possibly losing her big opportunity to shine. She placed individual self-interest above that of the team, and her overinflated ego was only complemented by her fourth major failure, which was a lack of trust.

Lisa's trust levels sucked bad—real bad—which was probably just a byproduct of the culture in which she was raised. The CIA is not exactly known for its transparent way of life and willingness to share information. Keeping her information close and *not* sharing it was how she was raised throughout her career. To trust someone or something to produce high quality work after never having worked beside them before is a difficult undertaking for anybody, but it must be done and it takes *courage* and self-confidence to do so. Lisa chose not to learn the fundamentals of purpose, passion, character, competence, family, and service—and she failed.

Organizational Competence

Organizational competence is derived from the people that facilitate the company's output, such as the analysts who collect market data and make invaluable projections, the managers who contribute to the growth of their employees, and the leaders who stay out of their people's business and focus more on the *overall* business.

But "smarts" alone will only take you so far without the collaborative efforts of others. Lisa was plenty smart, but she wanted her own cake and didn't want to share any bites. I know plenty of knowledge hoarders who don't say anything until the right people are in the room and then...*wham*! All of a sudden, they have diarrhea of the mouth and spit out facts, figures, theories, names, and everything else they know just to demonstrate how smart they are.

While it is certainly important to create a pool of talent and knowledge, its accumulation alone doesn't automatically create value for three reasons:

1. Employees with valuable information may not share their expertise with management because they assume that since *they* know something to be true, then everyone else must, too.

2. There is no communicative structure in place for people *to* share information, or the structure is ineffective.

3. There is no personal challenge for employees to apply unused talent, and so their skills and know-how deteriorate and become obsolete.

Competence is what you *know*. How you choose to apply it depends on your judgment, such as practical application, interpersonal connection, and improvement of cognitive or theoretical construct.

Nobody is born competent. In fact, my dad had a great quote on this subject. It was "everybody is born stupid." One must learn how to become a skilled doctor, firefighter, or salesperson, and the only way such knowledge is learned is if a person is humble and open enough *to* learn. There must be an eager desire to answer one's burning curiosity and a willingness to adopt it as "right."

Testing for Competence

In the SEAL Teams, those who did not meet the physical, mental, or emotional standards were kicked out. It was as simple as that. More often than not it was performance-based, but every once in a while there was a character flaw that garnered an immediate boot in the ass out the door. Depending on personality and cultural suitability, skills could be learned—but only if a certain baseline of competence existed, as well as core values like character and service. An individual had to prove that he *wanted* to be there, and he did this by volunteering for everything. The more he volunteered, the more he would learn and, consequently, the more competent he would become. Conversely, if someone displayed a character flaw such as lying, poor integrity, or "shady" behavior, he was immediately expelled. There was no room for a lack of trust in this environment—or anywhere for that matter. If you cannot trust the person you are working with in a highly dynamic and demanding environment, then that person shouldn't be there. Who you are as a person represents what the team and organization stand for, and why clients buy into your brand—or not.

Unfortunately, not all commands within the SEAL community shared this practice for the simple fact that "it's a numbers game." Some Teams simply choose not to flush away their Team Guy turds and instead sweep them under the rug, and those leaders guilty of this practice are the cannibalistic beings who eat away at our community from the inside, contributing to the denigration of their own community simply because bureaucracy says so.

The C2 Test

There is something I call the C2 test, which is the mutually-supporting value that character and competence bring to an individual's personal effectiveness. It's something that is assessed every day, in every training evolution, and every situation—inside of work and out. I have seen teams whose core values highlighted trust, integrity, and loyalty but to me, these values should be expected. That is, if trust, integrity, and loyalty are ideals that every employee should aspire to, then what's the standard at the time of hiring? Since today's global workforce faces increasingly complex challenges, greater emotional capacities and practical abilities are needed to anticipate more, and to tolerate the dynamic changes that pressure our everyday lives.

Concluding Thoughts

Chaos can strike at any time, and for myriad reasons. By its very nature—by definition—chaos remains undefined, and that's why people fear it. The reality is, though, that chaos can be managed—and in some cases, mitigated—through the development of curiosity that builds greater competence on both the individual and organizational levels. Develop your own competence, be vigilant not to fall into complacency, stay curious, and you'll be poised to adapt when the moment and situation call for it. Additionally, help to foster the adaptability of your own organization by encouraging cross-pollination, and push yourself to broaden your understanding beyond the confines of your own silo. You—and your organization—will be stronger for it.

The Second "C" of Chaos:
Character and Confidence

If there is one quality to look for in an aspiring job applicant, one quality that separates him or her from the rest, it's attitude. Skills can be learned, competence can be gained, but personality cannot. Some people are just born a-holes.

Attitude is a direct reflection of who you are. It reveals your disposition toward adversity, your openness to learning, how well you work with others, and how willing others are to work with you. I cannot think of a more simple recruiting process than hiring for attitude.

If you are familiar with Ernest Shackleton's historic journey in the early 1900s to cross Antarctica in hopes of reaching the South Pole, then you understand the value of having the right people. If this story is new to you, here is a brief summary of the grueling expedition.

Hiring For Fit: A Lesson in Employee Selection

Shackleton's goal of being the first explorer to trek across Antarctica was shattered when his ship, the *Endurance*, became wedged in the ice and his all-volunteer crew had to abandon ship. For almost two years in the unforgiving climate of Antarctica, the *Endurance* crew fought a battle of survival minute-by-minute among subzero temperatures and diminishing supplies; ultimately, Shackleton decided to split his crew into two groups—one to make an attempt to find help, the other to remain in a camp the crew had erected on the ice. The search party used the ship's lifeboats to journey toward the outer islands, where they trekked across land and eventually found a whaling station that provided rescue. Incredibly, every single person endured the two-year catastrophe.

Now, imagine the challenge that Shackleton—as a leader—had to face every minute of every day to sustain not only the morale, motivation, and hope of survival for his crew, but also for himself. The decisions, emotional stress, and uncertainty of the situation that he and his crew faced were certainly tested under the most extreme circumstances, and not to be directly compared to business of today. However, aren't those same capacities—physical, mental, spiritual, and emotional—not equally as important for all challenging situations, of any scale?

Additionally, while Shackleton's leadership was nothing short of remarkable during the hourly fight for survival, what was even more noteworthy was how he enticed volunteers to actually buy into his mission in the first place.

In order to fulfill his undertaking, Shackleton needed to solicit people who *believed* what he believed—people with no appetite for glory, fortune, or fame, but rather those who embodied the higher order ideals of honor, respect, and achievement. Shackleton only sought people who truly *wanted* to explore because if extreme hardship were to surface—as it did—then anybody who was less-than-willing to endure would only become dead weight. In other words, he needed the right cultural *fit*. To do so, he posted a "help wanted" sign for volunteers that read:

Men wanted for hazardous journey. Small wages, bitter cold, long months of complete darkness, constant danger, and safe return doubtful. Honor and recognition in case of success.

Shackleton's advertisement honestly communicated what was to be expected of the mission, with praise and fulfillment serving as the only rewards. Although Shackleton chose men with technical expertise, he was sensitive to having the right moral character and personality. He held temperament, optimism, and perseverance as vital ingredients to reaching success, and an equal balance of personalities on board, ranging from optimists to pessimists, was something he believed would aid in tackling such hardship.

What is so interesting here is the hiring process that Shackleton used to attract, select, train, and retain high potentials, because after the crew returned to their homeland, Shackleton set sail on another adventure with many of the same adventurers who had *just endured* that catastrophic journey. The underlying message of the "help wanted" sign already suggested the type of character and competencies that Shackleton was looking for, and the words themselves painted a grim picture of the mission that he hoped would serve as mental preparation for the journey. The selected applicants were chosen for:

- *Shared beliefs and values*

- *Curiosity and enthusiasm*

- *Skill and will*

Shackleton interviewed people who he believed would "fit the mold" of someone undertaking such an arduous task, people who possessed the psychological aptitude to prevail in any circumstance, seeking only the *opportunity* to flourish with sound leadership to guide them.

The 100 percent success rate of survivorship from the antarctic journey demonstrates the value of both selecting the right person for the job, and having sound leadership that affords the opportunity that *enables* potential. Circumstances may hinder resources, but they do not take away *resourcefulness*—the creative capacity to discover and use new ideas.

Personal fit, in my experience, comes down to one's acumen in four different areas of intelligence:

1. **Social smarts**: getting along with others (i.e. not being a "social hand grenade")

2. **Emotional smarts**: self-awareness and self-management (being aware of the words you say, how they sound, and with whom you communicate; knowing when and how to listen)

3. **Cognitive/conceptual smarts**: the mental horsepower to understand and communicate subject matter in one's job description (i.e. know-*what*)

4. **Practical smarts**: turning "brains into brawn;" shifting mental gears from memorizing material to applying it

How SEALs Identify "Right"

For what it's worth, I'll offer what is considered a good fit for new guys coming into the SEAL Teams so you can compare our view of "right" to your own. I am by no means suggesting that this is the only correct way to onboard personnel. Rather, I just want to offer a basis of comparison for your own understanding. As a newcomer, one should:

- *Show your teammates/coworkers that you're willing and able to learn. You do this by asking for responsibility before it's delegated.*

- *Volunteer for every new task. If no task arises, think of ways to make the current task better. Whatever happens, you do not wait to be told what to do (leaders are proactive, and proactive people don't wait to be told what to do because they are already doing it).*

- *Anticipate the needs of your team/department/coworker. Volunteering to train and mentor new employees are ways to demonstrate leadership aptitude. Working from macro to micro, big to small, the mission/purpose of the company always comes first, and you work from big to small with the individual always coming last. Self-interest is always the smallest area of focus.*

- *Demonstrate competence in your job. Even if the job is as menial as taking out the trash or making coffee, do it to the best of your ability, be on time, and never complain.*

- *Offer help to anyone and everyone who needs it or doesn't need it. Just the simple act of saying, "Jeff, I'm not doing anything right now. Do you need help with anything?" demonstrates a "we" and not a "me" mindset.*

People are the only resources that supply companies with the ability to create ideas, develop and enhance relationships, and share knowledge. They are also the one aspect that every single company in the world shares in common as a manageable resource that they choose who onboards and who doesn't. No matter what business you are in, the type of person that undergoes your company's onboarding process is something that *you* (as an individual, team, or organization) permit or prohibit. Every other financial, physical, and cultural resource depends on the mental, social, and psychological talent of those people *after* they prove themselves worthy of bearing the company's name.

People drive results. Job competence is a skill that can be learned and developed by anyone and everyone in all walks of life: professionals, experts, ninjas, or whatever you aspire to be. Job competence begins with the passion to pursue a clear purpose, and with passion in place, job competence is enabled and reinforced by having the right people, processes, rewards, and structure. Good companies can become great. Great companies can become badass. Badass companies don't get anymore badass, but they can certainly offer the tools to make their employees more ninja-like by focusing on the one thing that makes the world go round: *people.*

Leadership succession plans, growth opportunities, autonomy, and decision-making all serve to attract and retain talent. From day one at my last SEAL command, if you are not somebody who current leaders envision as a future team leader, then there is no reason to keep you. Members must be promotable and developable because if they aren't, then they really have nothing to contribute and nowhere to advance. This is the purpose of selection.

"Great" cultures build purpose, accountability, trust, and openness, whereas toxic cultures breed selfishness, pessimism, and finger-pointing. People are attracted to organizations because of what they represent. The

SEAL Teams attracted me for the action. The thought of jumping out of planes and sneaking around while carrying a gun all seemed like a great idea at the time. But once I got into BUD/S, and eventually the Teams, I realized that there was more to the job than just the cool stuff I saw on TV. I was now part of something bigger than myself. I realized that there were like-minded individuals who shared a special purpose, and the camaraderie that accompanied this uniqueness was—and is—unrivaled. I realized in SEAL training that it was the *people* who made the SEAL Teams unique because nowhere else on earth do you find people who willingly accept misery with both humor and indifference. Once I became immersed in the lifestyle of constant training, learning, and competition, I knew that I would come out on the other end better than when I entered, and when I did choose to leave the service, I would have something unique to give back to my family, society, or anybody willing to listen.

"Earning Your Trident"

There is a saying in the Teams: "Earn your trident every day," which essentially means to continually strive for improvement and to never rest on one's laurels. If you let up, you fail. If you fail, you lose. If you fail in a gunfight, you die. It's simple math.

Specwar is an all-volunteer community, which means two things: one may quit at anytime, or one may be involuntarily volunteered out at any time because his performance or character sucks. There have been quite a few stragglers who slipped through the cracks of BUD/S somehow, only to arrive at the Team and get washed out for the simple fact that their character was subpar, their competence was below standard, or they just sucked at life (hey, it happens). A high-performance organization (HPO) does not lend itself to holding employees' hands or micromanaging their performance. Rather, HPOs perform at the tip of the spear because each person continually sharpens his or her aptitude, knowledge, and skillset.

Striving to become "better" tells people that you're perpetually motivated to improve, that there is always something else to strive for because you believe there is always room for improvement. Being *better* means you are constantly improving yourself, your team, your department, and your company because excellence is not an end-state; it's a *next-*state, a mindset of endless pursuit. Nobody can do this alone. It takes a willingness to trust others and know that they share the same character and competencies as you.

Organizational Trust: The Standard

Companies sometimes throw trust to the wayside and consider it a benefit to the company's culture rather than a foundational element. After all, if trust cannot be traded or invested (in the financial sense), then it must not contribute to bottom-line profitability, right? Unfortunately, this all-too-common viewpoint couldn't be further from the truth.

Move At The Speed Of Trust

When we (SEALs) enter a room for clearance, we trust that our buddy is going to cover our six o'clock when our backs are exposed. There is only so much space one person can "clear" at a time, and how fast your buddy can clear your backspace determines how fast the entire room is cleared.

A team, company, or organization only moves as fast as its slowest member is willing and able to learn and produce. If you do not trust that such a person can keep up with the flow, then time gets wasted and costs rise—as you tap your foot and wait. So, what do you do?

Identify the standard. No matter how "great" someone is personally, if he or she doesn't live up to the standards in terms of character or competence, then this person is simply not *fit* to perform. As mentioned earlier, skills can be learned. But there's a fine line between investing and over-investing in someone or something where returns are no longer salvageable. Trust comes from the people, processes, and structures in place that govern behavior and define organizational culture. Economic crises, business bailouts, Wall Street uncertainty, and government intervention—every single one has produced some sort of illicit behavior that almost makes trusting someone in business seem like an abstract ideological concept, a great idea in theory that's impossible in practice. But without trust, one's physical, mental, and emotional prowess will never be fully realized. There is obviously a strong need for trust within the SEAL Teams, as our lives depend on it. But such a high order value isn't relegated to only those whose *lives* are on the line. Personal livelihood is just as valuable. Everyone has a living he or she must protect, and if trust doesn't exist within one's network or culture, then his or her livelihood becomes threatened. Sustained superior performance, therefore, isn't just the qualitative output of an organization, but a characteristic of the culture.

A Culture of Trust

In SEAL training, students must trust that the safety of the evolution resides within the competence of their instructors. Fear and uncertainty pervade every boat crew and individual—that's what BUD/S is about. The students who choose to endure, learn, and trust their instructors are the ones who will come as close to invincibility as they will ever know. Ignoring all else outside of their singular focus, their purpose-oriented minds become too powerful to be swayed or defeated. Because they trust themselves and have the self-confidence to tackle the unknown, facing ambiguity with conviction, these are the students who learn to embrace change. These warriors-in-training thus begin to morph their psyches into believing that anything is possible.

The only way trust is earned is by matching one's words to his or her actions. The concept of trust comes from an indisputable social rule: trust is only built if you are honest and tell the truth. This is achieved by:

- *Sharing your observations and insights*

- *Aligning your behavior with your words*

- Not *being a complete asshole*

Trust is essential to building enduring connections with employees, suppliers, customers, and the community. Nobody wants to work in an office where you don't trust the person next to you, nor is it ideal to work for a boss who doesn't extend opportunities *to* trust. Honesty and ethical behavior therefore create trust because the best way to spread an idea, value, or behavior is to live it. My first learning lesson of how to use trust as a tool for improvement came during the second phase of BUD/S and proved to be an exceptional method for surfacing individual character, as the next chapter will show.

Ethos

Character is who you are; competence is what you can do. My dad always used to say, "*Who* you are speaks louder than *what* you say. Now stop farting in public and help bag these groceries."

Character, or *ethos*, defines the person. Values like trust, integrity, authenticity, and humility are qualities that define who you are as a person, and they're the reason why people either value or avoid you.

The Naval Special Warfare community works on an honor system based on its members' ethos. Ethos defines who you are, the culture you're a part of, and what you—and therefore your company—stand for. One's ethos is comprised of the specific values that govern one's attitudes, behaviors, and beliefs. Your company's ethos either retains or dissuades the interest of employees based on the ideals and reputation the business holds.

In SEAL training, ethos represented a shared vision—a vision to which the volunteers had to subscribe, through a rite of passage known as BUD/S, if they wanted to fulfill their life endeavor. Those who chose not to endure this selective rite would never experience the power that such a close-knit community offers, and those who did discovered an uncommon level of respect and decency among teammates that most organizations can only envisage. Implicitly, each SEAL knows and practices not just a hard work ethic, but also honesty and selflessness; combined with a fundamental "we" mindset, these values comprise the basis of the SEAL ethos. The ethos that defines a special operator is a simple matter of choice. We choose to undergo a rite of passage that molds us forever, and this choice stems from the burning passion deep in our hearts and minds to pursue an inner calling—the calling of a purpose that "pulls" us into the skirmish that fights out of brotherhood.

However, enduring this rite doesn't necessarily eliminate the inequities with which every man lives. Inside every human being exists the potential to lie, cheat, steal, or just be a downright dirtbag, as some SEALs have undoubtedly demonstrated. But the people with whom you surround yourself ideally possess a collective goodness that suppresses any internal demons, and reminds you of who *you* are, why you're there, and what the team stands for. There is nothing worse than letting a teammate or family member down—especially when he or she believes in you and supports what you personify.

The "special" component of special operations reflects the organizational *fit* of each person (character) and the professionalization of the force (competence). The men selected to become special operators are chosen based on their physical, mental, and emotional capacities during a grueling selection process. Trainees demonstrate not just an ability to survive but also the ability to thrive in the face of adversity and personal challenge. Those who *choose* to adapt and overcome hardship are the sorts who define not just SOF, but any high-performing organization as it builds its own legacy—a mythos of uniqueness that attracts future talent.

Mythos

The mysticism of the SEAL persona—the belief that we hold our breath for hours at a time or that we need to kill a tiger shark in training—can be a self-fulfilling prophecy. There are the guys who only aspire to the SEAL Teams for the mystique of the action movie SEAL hero, and then there are the true warriors who only want to go to war and kick ass. The former are toxins, as their behavior and arrogance supersede the foundation upon which the real SEAL community is based, and compels them to exemplify the image that the public perceives rather than practice the ideals and values that define us. However, having said that, a mystical aura certainly serves a purpose because it attracts talent. Truthfully, the badass SEAL *mythos* was what enticed me to enlist—but as I mentioned, it was the teammates with whom I shared a purpose—the SEAL *ethos*—that kept me going.

Core values remain constant over time because they are just that—a concrete framework that supports a solid structure from which an individual derives his or her *being*. Values are fundamental, and without fundamentals there is no base to build upon.

The saying that my dad used to say—"Who you are speaks louder to me than what you say"—communicated to me the value of qualities that remain constant over time such as integrity, honesty, courage, and humility—qualities that are expected of others by those who already possess them, and unexpected by those who do not. Most importantly, the saying told me that people observe who you are through every move you make—or don't make—which lends itself to a focus on self-awareness and personal improvement.

How to Adopt the Fundamentals

How do you *hone* the abstract ingredients of purpose and passion, or character and humility? By exemplifying them every day in every decision that you make. In college, exercise became an addiction, something that I needed to do because it kept me on my path toward BUD/S. Working out was a tool that gave my daily routine meaning and reminded me that I was working toward a greater cause. In other words, fitness kept me aligned toward my purpose, and it became a part of who I was and what I learned to value. The *ideal* of fitness, though, doesn't just reflect physical exercise, but rather an adherence to and implementation of the values that guide you.

Here's what I mean. As a new employee entering a company, your focus is very myopic; it is self-focused by manner of necessity, because in order to survive you need to learn the ropes of the business and its culture, as well as the skills and competencies associated with your new job role. But as you begin to move up the organizational totem pole and into a position of management, your organizational aperture widens to the extent that there is less of a "me" and more of a "we" focus. This works fine until you move up into a position of leadership, where you must readjust your focus again to an eye exclusively on "we" as you move the pieces of the company puzzle around and place them into the greater whole. Resulting from this readjustment? You're left with almost zero "me" time. Leadership is *the hardest part* because it is time consuming, strategic, and covered with difficult decisions. As a result of leading others more, you are forced to lead yourself less. The values that were once important to you such as health, fitness, personal improvement, and mentorship—all of the things that helped shape the leader you are—begin to subside. In their place, over time, more "important" things begin to arise: the busywork of your increased responsibilities. So what happens? Those same values you once honed on a daily basis don't get the exercise that they need, and you start to become less of who you were.

Personal values, passion, family time, and humility will disappear if they are not reinforced, much like the technical skills associated with personal competence. If you don't subscribe to your own values, then why should anybody else? And if you are not doing what is important to you, then why should your people? The opportunities to practice them spring up out of nowhere at the most inopportune times as a means to test your will, unless you create them. Consider these occasions a gift.

How to Hone Character in the Workplace

Leo Widrich, cofounder of social media sharing platform Buffer, highlights the value of transparency in the workplace as a competitive advantage because of the trust it fosters among employees, helping them to understand *why* decisions are made. You see, Buffer goes to the extent of posting the salary and equities of each employee in plain view for the rest of the company to see, and then using a formula to determine compensation for current or future employees. The payoff is that people know exactly where they stand—and why. They see that there are no hidden deals between executives or wink-wink, nod-nods over compensation issues. The result, as Widrich claims, is "an incredible bond of trust among the team."

However, numbers and cents are just the tip of the iceberg at Buffer. Employees also share lessons learned, such as workplace challenges and solutions for improvement—a sort of after-action review (AAR) that will be covered in upcoming chapters.

Trust is difficult to establish, but even harder to reestablish, which is why Buffer's practice of transparency continually reinforces the ethos to which it subscribes. However, Buffer isn't the only company that hones its values on a daily basis. Google has an actual *transparency report* that is published online, displaying any and all information requests with regard to its Internet search engine.

I remember being in theater—Iraq and Afghanistan—with an open door policy for anyone who wanted to attend a briefing of any kind. Intel briefings, for instance, are normally reserved for senior officials or people who simply *need* to know, but our task force knew that with the constantly changing dynamics of the war, it wasn't good enough for team members to just know what to do; they had to understand why. If, on an objective, for instance, a team member hears a name, a location, or a face that triggers an association back to what he heard in the briefing, then he just built greater context to make more associations. Understanding how and why the car engine works is more important than knowing there's an engine under the hood; the former enables action, whereas the latter precludes it.

Summary

Character defines who you are and what your organization stands for. It's your brand, and brand reflects a promise of what you bring to the table and stand for in the long run. I wholeheartedly believe that people *want* to accomplish that which they set out to do. People want to perform well; they want to triumph. Character is who you are; competence is what you can do. Values like trust, integrity, authenticity, and humility are qualities that define who you are as a person and why people either value or avoid you. But they don't determine *what* you can do or how well your performance will be. Character must be interlinked with competence if you want to be a superior performer; otherwise, too strong a character turns into too much confidence, and that's when complacency sets in.

Filling the Knowledge Gap: Curiosity

The biggest obstacle to learning something is the belief that you already know it.
—Zen saying

Discontent is the first step in progress. No one knows what is in him till he tries, and many would never try if they were not forced to. There is nothing quite like ignorance combined with a driving need to succeed to force rapid learning.
—Ed Catmull, *Creativity, Inc.*

Chaos abounds as a firefight rages on the ground. To the strategic leader flying at twenty-five thousand feet, the situation on the ground doesn't look so bad. From your vantage point down in the trenches where you're getting shot at, however, you would beg to differ; all you can think about is why the hell the leader up high isn't helping.

You're in survival mode, the critical and sacred space where the inclination to find a solution is ever looming. It's the breaking point, where whatever you've always done isn't working for you anymore. You've brought down the risk of the known unknowns, but with the unknown unknowns erupting all around you, hunkering back down into what has always worked isn't going to cut it anymore. And when you're already in hell, searching for a way out that doesn't involve going back the way you came, curiosity steps in. Curiosity: what drives us, guided by purpose, back into the gap where the unknown lies—where we can discover for ourselves how best to bridge it.

It's only when the impetus for change is greater than the complacency not to that we become curious and begin to seek answers. However, when the status quo is acceptable, the push toward transformation declines. Curiosity dwindles. Comfort levels rise. The impetus to learn and grow subsides as one rationalizes what's *needed* and what's *desired*. See figure below.

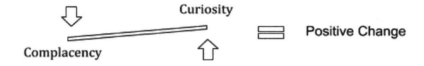

So, what is the secret to keeping the fire of curiosity burning? Purpose. Purpose is the key; it's the fuel that keeps the fire of curiosity burning because it continually poses the question, "Why?" When you're driven by a deep sense of purpose, you are able to meet new obstacles with conviction, adapting and overcoming to find a solution. It's a willingness to run into the fray against a known discomfort and deal with uncertainty head-on that defines one's true sense of curiosity—and purpose.

Self-awareness is what encourages your level of curiosity to fill the gap between certainty and uncertainty. If you're unwilling to be uncomfortable, then you're not willing to win; if you're not willing to tackle change and ambiguity, then you're not ready for new ideas to emerge. Until you're humble enough to embrace the unknown for what it is, ideas, creativity, and innovation are limited—because you are. The most inspiring leaders embrace the unknown because they know they don't have all the answers.

They're curious and they're humble enough to admit it. It's only when you admit to knowing less that you actually learn more.

If you want to sustain superior performance and navigate chaos, try listening to a three-year-old. Seriously. The curiosity those little suckers have is endless because they're constantly asking "why," they're always searching for answers to ambiguity, and as a result, they continually learn and grow.

As adults, we solve for ambiguity by staying curious as our ability to solve depends on our physical, mental, emotional, and spiritual capacities. Curiosity is what *enables* these capacities to thrive as you become better equipped to *choose* competence.

The greater your curiosity, the wider your angle of view and the more of the competitive environment you're able to see. Take, for example, former Air Force Colonel John Boyd, widely known for the OODA loop process of decision-making that he adopted from his learning experience flying fighter planes.

During the Cold War, dogfighting was the art of aerial battle—a practice less common today due to the technological advances over the years. What Boyd noticed as a pilot was this: while the soviet mig fighter was smaller, faster, and more agile than the overly cumbersome and slower American fighter plane, the mig typically lost in an aerial dogfight.

Why?

Because of the pilot's limited vantage point. Boyd realized that the mig pilot's narrow field of vision restricted him from anticipating the American fighter jet's next move simply because he couldn't see it. The US plane, conversely, had a much wider field of view, which enabled him to see more and, hence, beat the soviet fighter to the punch. Thus, Boyd discovered that the first person to successfully navigate the process of observation, orientation, decision, and action (OODA) would win. Every time.

What Boyd did was merge his previously-held knowledge and experience of flying with the *why* of the problem. In other words, Boyd stepped back from his street-level view of the problem and onto a balcony that overlooked the street—an alternative vantage point that enabled him to see more and, ultimately, build competence as a result.

When you understand how a new territory is oriented, you can better sift through the complexity of the competition. You see patterns emerge. Previous models that worked in other situations may not work with the current problem, but a modification might. Even if past changes resulted in so-called failures, what really matters is how you and/or the organization *learns and adapts* from such mistakes; how well you turn near misses into current-day building blocks that generate future success. This is how you beat the "migs" in your industry and stay relevant—by noticing what works, what doesn't, and treating "failures" not as exceptions, but rather launching platforms for innovation. The more thoroughly you understand your area of operations (AO) and how it's structured, the more prepared you will be to react when new threats emerge, and seize strategic opportunities.

Southwest Airlines

Southwest Airlines (SWA) is consistently considered one of the top five employers in the US by *Fortune, Forbes*, and *Business Insider* magazines, and one of the top companies in Jim Collins' *Great By Choice* due to its sustained superior performance in a complex environment. By complex, I am referring to uncontrollable, unpredictable, and rapidly changing circumstances that cause you or your organization to change. The difference between complex and complicated is this: complicated is solvable, whereas complex is ever changing, continually morphing, and therefore unsolvable. Complexity perpetually raises the bar every time you try to meet it, forcing you to either adapt or become obsolete. The only "solution" in a complex environment is to adapt—to implement a short-term pivot upon which future effectiveness can be built. Here's how Southwest did (and continues to do) it through the eyes of the OODA loop:

Observe

In order to compete amongst a sea of industry giants, SWA needed not just a value proposition, but a value differentiator; it had to distinguish itself from the big names of Delta and American Airlines. So, to do this, one must analyze the competition. What's the first thing you, as a consumer, notice about airline tickets? Pricing. Moreover, what is the main objective for many passengers when they travel? Pricing. In an effort to appeal to the masses, SWA's goal was (and still is) to offer the cheapest fare in the business. Period.

Other observations SWA made about the competition included:

1. *Ticket cost (number and type of aircraft)*
2. *Number of industry options (for low cost fares)*
3. *Customer satisfaction*
4. *Worker efficiency*
5. *Airports used*
6. *Routes used*
7. *Gate turnaround time*

Now, to carry out this objective, SWA needed to dig deeper. In other words, they had to...

Orient

Southwest's purposeful orientation toward the competitive landscape was exactly what put them on the map. By analyzing key performance indicators such as gate turnaround time, the size and type of aircraft fleet used by competitors, and customer satisfaction (measured through airport delays), SWA could more accurately predict their likelihood of success. With this data they were now in a position to...

Decide

Armed with the right information, SWA could now decide upon which performance indicators to build their value proposition upon, which I have compiled into three areas:

1. **Time.** SWA's gate turnaround time is approximately twenty minutes, which is faster than all other airlines in the airline industry. Additionally, while other airlines flew from one airport hub to another, SWA employed direct flights, which minimized lost baggage and improved travel time.

2. **Resources.** While competitors had to operate, maintain, and repair a plethora of diverse aircraft models, Southwest chose to use a single type (737) for everything. Furthermore, since SWA only flew point to point, they didn't need extra staff for baggage transfer.

3. **Requirements.** With a single aircraft used company-wide, Southwest could streamline the requirements (and therefore costs) needed for onboarding new pilots and flight attendants. There were fewer instruction manuals to prepare, fewer training courses to conduct, and fewer spare plane parts to keep in inventory.

The key to decisions is to make the options simple to choose from, which is exactly what Southwest's strategy entailed.

Act

And act they did. As a result of Southwest's simple strategy, the airline giant boasted record-breaking streaks of profitability after reaching twenty years of sustained performance in 2001.

Just as the American fighter pilots saw their competitive landscape better, so too did Southwest Airlines.

Learning and Change

Change requires learning, and learning requires change. It is a reciprocal and inextricably linked relationship, as change—personal or organizational—necessitates the adoption of new processes, motives, rules, and relationships, while also letting go of their antecedents.

Following the shoot, move, and communicate example introduced earlier in this book, you will recall that to *move* is to alter one's position, mindset, or emotions—be it organizationally, personally, or professionally. Change often has a negative connotation because it implies something involuntary—a *push* toward the edge of the cliff—simply because of the unknown black hole in which *change* resides. People resist change and resist being changed. That's no secret. But without change, there is no learning and no evolution—only complacency, and, ultimately, chaos.

The Value of Humility and Learning in Sustaining

Superior Performance

Entering a room of an enemy target is nerve-racking to say the least—but it's incredibly addictive. The thrill of being at the threshold of uncertainty is inexplicable to anyone who hasn't done it, but the leadership principles involved are common to all.

Room entry tactics differ according to the threat level of the target. Generally speaking though, each assaulter has a direction in which he is to go, and the direction he chooses determines the action of the teammate behind him.

The doorway itself is known as the "fatal funnel," as that's the first reference point any inhabitants inside the room focus on and, consequently, aim their muzzles at. The goal, then, is to get away from the doorway as quickly as possible. If a teammate were to freeze in the doorway out of hesitation, trepidation, or uncertainty, he would immediately be putting not only himself at risk but also the rest of the team because the element of surprise would be gone. What such trepidation really indicates, however, is self-interest. When the individual instinct for self-interest is placed above that of the team or the organization, it doesn't matter whether the context is military or business, because chaos will ensue.

In the business world, if an employee chooses self-interest over the mission of the company, then the entire organization is placed at risk. How? Trust erodes as backstabbing grows; communication channels implode because trust is no longer there; micromanaging becomes the flavor of the day because trust levels are so low and communication channels no longer exist. Consequently, decision-making worsens and a leader's plate is heaped with additional roles and responsibilities. The desire to put oneself above all else reveals a lack of shared purpose.

To stay competitive, companies must change; they must adapt over time. But, they can only adapt at the speed of *learning*. If *moving* is akin to adaptability (i.e. change), then learning only comes after one has disconfirmed previous knowledge and internalized and processed new information. Before one moves, in any regard, the "old" must be accepted as "out" and replaced with the "new" (or "right" information). Otherwise, adaptation doesn't occur.

Learning takes place when you humbly acknowledge that the information you once knew to be "right" is now obsolete, and you trust the source of that new information to be accurate. This concept makes humility and trust extremely significant components to adaptability, because they are what allow us to welcome new opportunities.

But once this new information is adopted, it must be shared with the team. Knowledge is only as good as what the individual with that information actually does with it, as there are plenty of brilliant people out there who can recite the encyclopedia but put their shoes on backwards because they don't know how to apply what they know. What happens at that point is this information is (mis)interpreted by others who see the problem as *they* see it rather than how the organization sees it. Then chaos ensues.

Information drives decisions, so there can't be any confusion or obscurity in the information itself, or the roles and responsibilities of the person managing that information. Learning must be transparent across the organization if you want to minimize the peaks and valleys associated with organizational change.

Organizational Change: Learning to Summit the Peak

Picture the last mountain you climbed. If this example doesn't apply to you, then just envision the next mountain you want to climb. From the bottom of the mountain you can see the peak, which is your destination. You start climbing, but as you progress higher and higher, you become more inundated with the everyday processes and "urgencies" that arise; a zig here, a zag there, and the peak becomes less visible. There are more and more paths and trails that zig and zag that take your focus off the peak. There may even be fifteen different times where you *think* you have arrived at the peak, only to find yet another path—another "urgency"— that tells you, "you're not there yet—here's one more thing to do." So you keep climbing diligently while, at the same time, continually spotting new pathways and alternate routes that all point "up" in the direction you want to go. Progressing in this way, you either tough it out, maintain focus, and summit the peak (i.e. overcome change); or you give up, say "this is too much," and turn around.

To reach any high point, there must be strong leadership to steadily challenge the central values, ideas, processes, and activities that govern the culture. Overseeing this process, the leader needs to be someone who aims to share his or her knowledge with others by constructively questioning their own.

Sharing information fuels the knowledge gap and enhances both your position and that of the company's in five unique ways:

1. Employees are now "armed" with the right information so they can solve their own problems more efficiently.

2. A "borderless" culture enriches cohesion and coordination.

3. A standard is created to which people may hold themselves, and others, accountable.

4. It leaves a legacy such that critical information and "best practices" are passed down through the years.

5. Individual performance improves. Make no doubt about it. The mission and team come first, but the individual's character and competencies are what makes the team—and the mission—possible.

AARs

Organizational fitness is about how a company's collective capacity to perform over time compares to that of their competitors, with the more "fit" one emerging as the victor. Sustaining superior performance, though, requires more than just a retrospective lens. In other words, increased performance means never settling, and therefore, always learning. Together.

The concept of *moving* entails a constant shift from one level of preparedness to another, as it is perpetual learning and improvement at its finest. The means by which we did this as a team was through after-action reviews (AARs).

AARs were conducted after every major training block and certainly every mission, with the objective of exploring what was supposed to happen, what actually happened, and why. In other words, AARs were open discussions that allowed us to discover, uncover, and recover knowledge. Members contributed their own personal perspectives about the mission based on their night's experience and their own actions. This shared learning environment thus allowed every other participating member to better assimilate individual action with organizational intent. For instance, the pattern recognition of one team member would enlighten the pattern recognition of junior members such that if a similar situation were to arise (which always did), then their response time to observe, orient, decide, and act (OODA) shortened. Decision making speeds up, response times slow down, the enemy goes down. Boom.

AARs reinforced interdependencies among the team because each member knew—*better than before*—what everyone else is likely to do the next time. Members became more apt to anticipate *potentially* critical events before they unfold because they now have a collective attention directed toward the same problem.

The key aspect of the AAR is the honesty and strict focus with which they're conducted. The more detail and attention to results, the higher the expectations for improvement the next time. Perfection in execution thus becomes a norm that is internalized as the focus of each member is on improvement. What arises is an expectation to perform up to the issues talked about in the last AAR session because nobody wants to be "that guy" who repeats a previously observed mistake. If he did so more than once, then his value to the team was reassessed.

Such a systemic understanding of each member's role and responsibility to the team reduces the potential for organizational blind spots. Sports commentators are mostly former professional athletes themselves, which means they can offer insight because they *know* the sport. A former coach who has seen the macro picture will have a greater understanding of roles and responsibilities, strategies, and contingencies than a player who has played in one role his whole life. Similarly, the vice president who grew up in sales probably has a greater perspective on the business as a whole than the VP with no sales experience.

Even the smallest detail is considered a topic of scrutiny during an AAR because of the high stakes involved. For instance, in a high-risk environment where the risks are absolute and second chances are nonexistent, a "significant" learning lesson would likely reflect a behavior, a decision, or a response that garnered a fatal consequence—which is not ideal. Operating through the sea, air, and land, for example, poses a danger at every level, beginning with the operator and spreading upwards into the upper echelons of leadership. When you run a high-performing team and everyone is a star, success is expected—but never assumed—because what comes with high-stake triumphs are limited margins for error—and thus very granular learning lessons.

Nobody ever learns from a success like they do from a failure. Only through failure do lessons become deeply ingrained in our minds as either a "don't do this again" or "this is awesome!" mental note, where the former sparks a negative emotion that tells the brain not to repeat whatever it was that just happened, and the latter pulls you toward repetition. Since the price we, as SEALs, pay for failure is oftentimes the difference between life and death, there are fewer opportunities for *deeply* significant learning to occur. Thus, to keep the gap between failure and success as close as possible we must tweak and fine-tune even the smallest occurrences or *potentials* for failure.

It always takes something close to a boot in the ass to drive a lesson home—for me, at least. Take, for example, a constant winning streak where a coach, player, parent, or employee doesn't see the value in closing the gap between failure and success. Too much of anything can change a team's attitude, constrict their awareness about strengths and weaknesses, cause them to make unhealthy assumptions, or get comfy with the way things currently work. The problem here is that people derive self-efficacy and competence from the *act* of winning, rather than looking at *why* their performance almost crossed the line into the "loser" category. They say, "Wow, we barely escaped that one, but we won!" instead of digging deeper into *why* the team even got close to failure in the first place. The tendency is to put up one's feet up and attribute victory to competence, rather than study the line between winning and losing that almost shaped their future. Learning opportunities thus wash away and performance ultimately stagnates, as the team becomes a self-licking ice cream cone.

AARs focus on the next area of improvement by shortening the gap between failure and success, such that *complacency* and *chaos* are minimized and *curiosity* is maximized. There are two ways to view a "win." After the first time I was shot, for example, I perceived the situation as a failure on my part for the simple fact that I presented myself to the enemy. However, it was a success because I walked away and the enemy didn't (which I attribute to my shooting buddy, incidentally, not me). However, it was also a failure because that insurgent should never have had the time to even get those shots off, and *that* was the part that I—we—had to analyze, the *why*. Any success that is close enough to failure should be considered an area for development. Many people wonder how we, as SEALs, can routinely solve impossible situations where the stakes are so high. The answer lies in part with the AAR and the level of ruthless scrutiny to which we subject ourselves: sustaining "close to" superior performance doesn't count, and anything less than superior warrants a discussion for improvement.

This perspective goes against the grain of traditional opinions, where one may consider a near miss as proof of how "good" he is or how reliable the system has proven. If your perspective is the latter, then when a true mishap occurs it will be too late to fix it. There's a quick way to determine how you and your company deal with failures and near misses. Ask yourself this question: "What happens when a mistake is made?" Do people come together and work through the issue collaboratively? Or, do they ignore the issue altogether or stiff-arm the perpetrator like a bad habit?"

There are a few other key aspects of AARs that are worth noting because they help define the character and competency of the organization. The first is an indifference to rank. With the purpose of the AAR being improvement, in order to dissect the mission and candidly communicate in ways that make *the team* better, everyone must be held to the same standards and expectations of performance. From the lowest-ranking enlisted up to the highest-ranking officer who took part in the mission, everybody must be held accountable for not only his actions but the actions of his immediate teammates as well. One key point of the forum's openness is that discussions do not challenge a participant's self-efficacy. There must be a dividing line between person and position so as not to attack one's individual self-worth. Rather, there's a higher purpose. Members are there to learn why actions and decisions unfolded as they did and consider ways for improving the next mission.

The second defining aspect of an AAR is facing conflict. When a decision or behavior was made that affected the entire team, members needed to know why that decision was made. Dissecting such issues forces people to be accountable for their choices and actions—as well as others. The open forum builds team trust because everyone is transparent about what happened and the purpose that drove their behavior. Candor is praised because it connotes character. If a team member could've asked for help but chose not to, then he is seen as incompetent, unaware, not a team player, or a combination of the three. At any rate, there was a serious *character* issue to address. An area for development is seen as a holistic problem rather than an individual issue (unless the individual did something stupid that nobody else could've done). Mistakes must not be confined but rather shared to keep the links of the chain bound together and the force intact.

To become more competitive and continually drive innovation, we review everything—from mission conception to execution to post-op— and nitpick everything along the way with a strict focus on *why* things occurred the way they did. *Winning* was the mission because second place in our market was fatal, and everything was planned to facilitate organizational fitness at every level such that each member knew exactly what the others were doing and why they were doing it. *This* is how you enable success and remain at the top of your game—by communicating purpose, openly engaging in reflection, and sharing lessons learned from across the spectrum of the organization.

Be A Student Of The Game

Marshall Faulk, seven-time NFL Pro Bowler and three time First-Team All-Pro, has been considered one of the most influential offensive players of the game, not just for his skill, but for how he studied the game. Faulk saw context—patterns of behavior—that allowed him to anticipate the next moves of both the defense and his teammates, and therefore, he was able to make decisions faster. He understood the why that drove each player to act and how every member on the football field was just an individual "piece" that, taken as a whole, comprised a much larger puzzle. It wasn't Faulk's forty-yard dash time that made him play faster (although it probably helped), but rather his ability to lessen the gap between stimulus and response; the time it took for him to read and react.

If you or your team works in one organizational silo then your ability to "see" the playing field is very narrow. Even worse, it never grows. Key players miss critical insights that could have better shaped their decision-making.

Afghanistan, 2008: How Context Saved My Sweet Ass

During another rotation as a cross-functional team leader for a joint task force in Afghanistan, two other SEALs were assigned to me from SOCOM, who were absolutely incredible operators and people. Much like the situation described in previous chapters, my role was to work hand-in-hand with the CIA chief of base to action targets. We actually had a great relationship as compared to the volatile one I'd previously had with Lisa, but one night they (the CIA) just couldn't play. The agency had other commitments, which was fine, so we passed our target over to the Rangers on the condition that we participate as well.

The targeted individual was a known IED facilitator who just happened to live about eight hundred meters north of the Afghan-Pakistan border—a solid choice for a dwelling since he could ideally see or hear anything foreign coming from a mile away and consequently flee across the border, thus preventing us from further pursuit.

We inserted via helicopter about one kilometer north of the target—a less-than ideal distance. Surprisingly, no one was seen fleeing the compound until we got much closer. My team climbed the roof to cover down on activity inside the compound while the Rangers set an explosive breach on the exterior door. The charge went, blew the door, and the rangers made entry.

Meanwhile, another ranger element had set up south of the target just across a dried out river wadi to act as a catcher's mitt if anybody tried to flee from target. They also had slightly higher ground, and could therefore see the entire compound.

Of course, once the Rangers made entry, noise discipline was nonexistent. The gig was up, and an unknown male from the target chose to try and flee the assault force. Bad choice.

"Jeff, the second ranger element reports that someone just fled the compound heading south. He jumped into a ditch and hasn't reemerged."

Oh shit, we got a barricaded shooter, I thought. There was only one reason anyone with any tactical acumen—which had to be assumed—would take a position of lower elevation like a ditch, and that was because it wasn't really a "ditch" but a fortified trench that (likely) housed a cache of weapons. The way I saw it, the "ditch" was an emergency fallback created by the enemy for a situation just like this.

"Ok, we're on it," I radioed back to the sergeant. It was myself and four other guys—one of which was an interpreter whom I trusted wholeheartedly—and we maneuvered over toward the "ditch."

It was the year prior to this current deployment in Iraq (the first time I was shot) where a number of enemy situations shaped my perspective forever; they provided context for situations like this.

The Army had a general rule at the time that they followed for engaging enemy combatants: the weapons count must equal the body count. In other words, if an enemy killed in action (EKIA) did not have a weapon, then he or she must not have been a threat. The problem with this mindset is that war isn't black and white. It's gray. Even those leaders who attribute morality and ethics to wartime decision-making, my question for them is: when was the last time you were in this situation? When was the last time you faced a suicide bomber who "didn't have" any visible weapons on him? If, for example, they (Army) had never been exposed to the same fanaticism that we had—the "unarmed" suicide bombers or men dressed as women carrying anti-personnel mines—then sure, the rules of engagement (ROEs) may appear black and white. But they weren't. Like many things, ROEs are open to interpretation based on what one *interprets* as right and as a threat at the time.

The context that came to mind while approaching this "ditch" made my decision-making process simple: the first movement I see and positively identify as a threat, I am going to shoot in the face. Why? Because innocent people don't run.

I maneuvered the team to get on-line—vernacular for standing abreast of each other facing the same direction—and then gave the go ahead to move forward. The channel of dirt where the supposed ditch lay was slowly approaching.

So what's it going to be? I thought. *An AK? A grenade?* I was just waiting for a head or a gun to stick out, or a grenade to be thrown randomly in our direction. *That would be just my luck.*

Fifty meters…forty…

I looked left and right to ensure we were all still abreast of each other. You didn't want one guy to get too ahead of himself and cut down the field of fire for you or the team.

Twenty meters…fifteen…ten…

Just as we approached the trench, everyone on the team had different vantage points because the ditch formed a loose "S" shape. I slowly peered over the ridge and cleared the deadspace—scanned left to right, right to left—and didn't see anything.

Until…

On my secondary sweep to the left I noticed, through my night vision goggles, an abnormal shape on the ground about ten meters from my position. The shape resembled the same color as the ground but seemed to have a different texture; it couldn't have been sand because the outline didn't mirror anything natural. In fact, the more I traced with my laser from the top down, the more it looked like…

My eyes narrowed. As I said before, the things that come to mind in precarious situations are worthy of recording, because they cannot be mimicked or replicated. One voice in me asked, *What the fuck is that?* until the other—the more rational side—responded with, *I don't know. Shoot it.*

So that's what I did.

I pumped two rounds into this thing only to hear "Uhhhh."

My eyes turned into saucers. *Oh shit, that's a dude!* The outline I traced with my laser was now uncanny. There was no doubt that it was a guy hiding underneath a desert colored sheet in the middle of a four-foot deep trench. Who does this?

So I dumped about eight more rounds into the top of his head to ensure he wouldn't limp away or blow himself up.

After we deemed the ditch secure I went to conduct a sensitive site exploitation (SSE) on the him to see what he had on him as far as ID, weapons, explosives, intel, etc. After doing a remote pull to verify he wasn't lying on any grenades, I began a body search and came up with…uh oh.

Meanwhile, the fact that somebody shot a bad guy on a Ranger target was apparently a big deal, so the Ground Force Commander wobbled over to see what a dead bad guy looked like.

As he looked over the dead body, I heard him murmur to himself, "All rounds center mass. No weapon." I knew at that point there would be a problem; a battle over ROEs because this officer just didn't have the context of 1) getting shot in the plates like I did a year ago and 2) the run-ins we had with insurgents who were willing to kill themselves just to kill you, as upcoming chapters will attest.

Now, imagine what would happen if we replaced the Rangers and SEALs here with two different companies about to enter a merger. The difference in culture between the two organizations is huge and can cause enormous roadblocks and political catastrophes if context isn't shared. Rangers are elite infantry; SEALs are special operations. Rangers tend to be young, work in large numbers, and therefore necessitate greater instruction and protocol, which limits their ability to creatively solve problems. Each organization must work with the other. Each side must share knowledge to understand the *why* behind each other's decision-making. If they don't, then the enemy flees or, worse, you get buried.

What saved my sweet ass was the lessons I had learned from previous deployments, the unknown situations where the unexpected unfolded and completely redefined our ROEs. Sure, the logic that the body count must equal the weapons count is applicable *if* the enemy is using a rifle or pistol. But sometimes, however, it's a cell phone, a suicide vest that you can't see, a grenade under his armpit with the pin pulled such that when he puts his hands up, the grenade falls and kills him *and* you. Sharing this context with the Ground Force Commander was critical to not only explain my rationale for defense, but to enlighten him and his men for theirs.

Summary

When you offer *learning opportunities* to someone with both the passion and drive to succeed, the result is a highly competent individual.

Transparency is learning that bridges the gap across physical, social, and political boundaries, such as during an after-action review. It is what fuels sustained superior performance. While holding knowledge may be powerful, sharing knowledge is where real power lies. We therefore learned as a team *and* as an organization—rather than as individuals—and this was only possible because we shared the same purpose, derived the same meaning from the job, and respected the enemy enough to be quietly confident about our success.

To get on the same page there must be transparency such that everyone knows what the intended direction is. When information and daily routines are transparent, there are no surprises, the speed bumps are smaller, and summiting the peak appears feasible.

Competence is learned, as is curiosity and humility. One must learn how to become a skilled doctor, firefighter, or salesperson, and the only way such knowledge is learned is if a person is humble enough *to* learn, when trust exists between the sender and receiver, and when he or she is open enough to share.

Key Takeaways

- *After-action reviews facilitate knowledge transfer and breed an openness amongst members.*

- *Understanding why allows you to anticipate situations before they develop and enable more effective decision-making.*

- *Rely on what you know and what you can affect. If others don't have the awareness that you do, school them on it. You only have one shot to win.*

- *Mistakes—or areas for development, as I like to call them—happen. Deal with it. They are part of any learning process and the best thing to do is learn from such hiccups, share your experience, and become better—both personally and organizationally—because of them.*

Just When You Thought You Had Enough

Humility is not thinking less of yourself, it's thinking of yourself less.
—C. S. Lewis

There are few things in life that you can never have enough of. Food, money, and sex come to mind—although not necessarily in that order—but they're well outside the scope of this book. Though not as titillating or indulgent as the food/money/sex options, there are two more values that matter—a whole lot. These are curiosity and humility, virtues so important that I included an additional chapter to stress their significance. Moreover, if there's one thing that's oftentimes lacking, it's humility.

BUD/S is twenty-six weeks long and divided into three phases: physical conditioning, diving, and land warfare. You would think that by the time second phase rolled in, that a class would have fully confided in each other by then, gelled, and felt comfortable together.

Not our class.

About halfway through diving phase, our class had a problem—each other—and it was time to face the music.

The one element that we as a class lacked was accountability. We only worried about our own individual performances and failed to see how we were just smaller parts of a much bigger—and stronger—whole. Everyone was worried about having to run to the surf zone to get wet again (as if we wouldn't anyway), to do more pushups, or to swim buddy another student to the surf. The whole teamwork thing hadn't sunk into our self-occupied little minds yet, and we didn't realize that we were not there in BUD/S for ourselves, but rather, for a higher cause, a nobler purpose, and something that lives, breathes, and dreams *teamwork*.

Every student at this point had demonstrated unparalleled resolve and dedication to purpose since we had already survived hell week, but as a whole, we had failed to serve the interest of the class. Much like employees exist to serve their organizations, we existed (within the construct of BUD/S) to serve each other, and that was the only way we were going to make it through training.

Too often people forget what their purpose is. They think—selfishly—that they are employed to earn a profit, to make money, or to get their "kill" so that they can go home and do it again the next day. On a very micro level scale this may be true, but this is not why an employee exists in his or her organization. As stated earlier, employees exist to serve their organizations. Profits and dead bad guys are just the byproduct of the purpose you believe in.

Back to our BUD/S class…

How could we as a class have evolved sooner? More communication? Maybe. But we didn't trust each other enough *to* communicate more openly. In other words, we innately feared internal strife and disagreement with each other, which sounds silly in regard to men who aspired to become an elite fighting force, but it's really just human behavior.

Humans all face conflict and uncertainty within themselves, their families, and others at some point. Strangely, if the internal conflict within oneself lacks resolution, then oftentimes one's family and the people surrounding him or her are the ones who suffer. Facing and overcoming this personal chaos that drives our behavior is absolutely critical to finding certainty. SOFs and their families face physical, mental, and emotional challenges while training and deploying, and the ability to deal with such adversity must be harnessed to maintain any sort of sanity. The last thing anybody wants to deal with is a highly trained, highly motivated, and highly resourceful—and grumpy—commando.

One Friday in dive phase of BUD/S, an instructor sat in front of us in the second phase classroom after the day was over, and affectionately expressed his feelings: "I fucking hate this class." He said:

> *You guys don't work together. You don't care about each other. What I see are a bunch of individuals who just want to save their asses. We [the cadre] are not finished getting rid of you guys yet. I only want to work with guys who know how to work together as a team. If that means only one or four or ten or none of you graduate then so be it, because I am not sending garbage into the Teams. You guys need to figure out how you're going to gel before Monday morning, because if you all are not working together by then, then you all will have wished you'd quit, because the rest of BUD/S is really gonna suck.*

From there, the instructor walked out of the classroom, leaving us relieved that we didn't have to run into the surf to get wet and sandy, but at the same time feeling somewhat disappointed with ourselves. It was abnormal for an instructor to *really talk* to us. If he had punished us, then we could have just rationalized the situation as being part of BUD/S. But it wasn't. Instead, he spoke to us genuinely (as much as a BUD/S instructor could) and left us physically unscathed but morally wounded, which had an even stronger impact.

Well if we weren't fucked before, we're definitely *fucked now.*

In hindsight, it wasn't punishment at all. It was a wake-up call. The fact is that instructors will have to work with the students they put through training, which is a strong motivator to be held accountable and forge the men with whom they would enter battle.

What we as a class did next was a turning point in our BUD/S careers. I suggested that we publicly evaluate each other right then and there in front of our peers, because I had seen it done in a previous class and it worked. We needed to let the floodgates of criticism flow and our egos washed away from our self-righteous minds. No instructors present, just us. Everybody agreed, but with a few stipulations:

1.   Only one person could speak at a time.

2.   The senior man (the officer in charge) would serve as the moderator until it was his turn to go.

3.   The recipient would keep his mouth closed until the critic was finished speaking—thus forcing himself to listen.

Everything was on the table. We critiqued everything from poor work ethics, selfishness, and arrogance, to low integrity and even just generally "sucking" at life. Of course, those who garnered nothing but positive results were praised for their contributions to the class. Such a holistic approach embraced openness and forced guys to face conflict—and ultimately choose to model themselves after those who were held in higher regard. In doing so, we clearly outlined expectations and delineated roles. The stipulations painted a picture of what was about to come into everybody's mind so that each student could internalize what he was about to face and prepare himself mentally. It was, essentially, a clear—and shared—vision.

We all sat in the classroom at tables and chairs that were lined up facing a whiteboard and an eight-inch-high stage at the front of the room. The stage was elevated so that whoever was on it could look down over the class and collect everyone's attention.

The first volunteer climbed onto the stage and sat in a chair facing the class. Various members of the class raised their hands to indicate they had something to say and were called upon by the poor guy on stage. Class critics said something like, "I don't like how you shun work. It seems that you always disappear whenever there's work to be done. Like the other day…" Or, "In my opinion, you are consistently ranked at the bottom of the class for [these reasons]…" If a member was a solid performer, then he would be told to climb down off stage because nobody had anything for him.

What happened in the following days was incredible. Prior to this event, each member felt as if more and more air was being inflated into his emotional "tire" that, eventually, would pop. But this open and honest conjoining had allowed us to depressurize some of the air that had been building within. A large weight had been lifted off our shoulders because we all knew where each member stood, and we were more willing to talk about it. There was no more hiding out for those who shunned work or didn't volunteer as much as other guys. There was no more talking behind each other's backs, no more bullshit being slung, because now we felt comfortable openly addressing each other. After the class expressed its concerns, gripes, opinions, and complaints, an incredible thing happened.

We gelled.

We challenged each other's ideas. We left rank at the door. We avoided complacency by excavating the truth through a series of candid questions and answers. We also discovered personal accountability. Anybody who has ever worked in a team knows what it's like to gel or come together. There is a feeling of unbelievable efficiency and invincibility when you work beside someone who shares the same drive that you do. Misery loves company, but no one suffers when everyone shares the same definition of misery as everyone else.

We came together as a class because we were vulnerable with each other. We exhibited trust on many levels during this forum—within ourselves and amongst the class—that enabled us to communicate our deepest concerns with each other with no fear of reprisal. Nobody was scared to say what was on his mind because each one of us knew that in the grand scheme of things, there was a higher purpose to serve here—and worrying about hurting people's feelings wasn't it.

When you publicly communicate your beliefs and intentions, you make yourself public. You demonstrate vulnerability by doing so because, let's face it; nobody actually likes airing out their dirty laundry for others to see. But the "world," in this case, involves teammates who *should* be able to voice their concerns and ideas publicly, as doing so also has positive implications on human capital because:

1. ***It conveys responsibility and commitment to the cause.*** By publicly expressing one's concerns and/or ideas, it communicates to other participants that this person is a stand up guy and one that cares about the mission. In doing so, it also creates the perception of being a go-to guy for information because, for those who fear speaking up in public, they may choose to come to you to bring up their voices. It allows you to influence from the bottom-up by forming an alliance of shared interests.

2. ***It raises ideas and perspectives that others may not have previously considered.*** Sharing honest and unadulterated opinions in this context opens up the eyes of listeners and broadens their perspectives.

Students displayed courage in volunteering their critique of others and in receiving criticism. It takes "thick skin" to sit there and listen to thirty-some guys tell you why you may or may not suck. Now, I'm not suggesting that you run around and tell everybody *exactly* what you think of them as a best practice—there are certainly constructive ways to offer positive and negative feedback. But for us, this approach worked because of the shared vulnerability that was encouraged from the group and by the class leader. After all, receiving such candid feedback only served to improve ourselves and the class. What is so important about establishing trust is the reciprocal effect it has on both sides.

Looking back, there were three important lessons I learned from that Friday in the second phase classroom. First, that the condition—the environment—is more important than the people in it, as it's the environment that *shapes* behavior. You cannot tailor to individual motivations as your team or organization grows. Many of the change initiatives that companies undergo attempt to tailor to the personal desires of each employee, playing a game of personal favorites. What these endeavors resemble is a man-to-man defense. Remember playing man-to-man defense in sports? I remember, and it sucked. It was incredibly more tiresome to chase after one single player the whole game than it was to "stay in your lane" and manage your area, and that's what businesses need to adopt with respect to change.

In that second phase BUD/S classroom, we set an environment where trust and dialogue were the *expectations*. Not participating wasn't an option.

What we created in that space was a forum for openness, an opportunity for conversation in which we outlined expectations for honesty, listening, and dialogue. Accountability was the emergent property. We created the space *for* trust, which allowed us *to* trust. Trust propelled us forward because relationships—teamwork—depended on it. The open expression of that BUD/S instructor suggested authenticity and legitimacy. We *believed* that he was genuine and forthright and thus decided to heed his suggestion of finding a way to gel as a class—something that inspirational leaders do well.

Second, we created certainty from an uncertain situation simply by exposing our inner selves. We went from a group of individuals to a team as we subsequently shared a common vision that became a common purpose. Gaining a pledge from others begins with the courage *to* trust and reveal the authentic self. Without authenticity—without staying true to oneself—trust cannot be fostered. Nothing goes on in this world without relationships. *People* make the world go round. Whether it's business, marriage, or a seemingly "personal" issue, chances are it involves more than one personality, so there is a natural human component in everything we do. Relationships are everything. The missions that we receive as an SOF community are based off the rapport established with the Department of Defense, Department of State, battle space commanders, local governments, and any indigenous forces *with* whom we work. We do not work alone, save special circumstances. Special operators are used (willingly) as pawns in a much larger strategic chess game by senior decision makers who *choose* to use us *because* they believe in us, and the only source these policy makers have to buy into our capabilities comes from the leaders who *communicate* our character and competence as a community to *make* those policymakers believe in us.

The last important lesson I learned that day in BUD/S was that scorpions are scorpions and frogs are frogs (no pun intended). People don't change. Instead, they choose.

The Scorpion And The Frog

A scorpion wanted to cross the stream, but being a scorpion, he couldn't swim. So he scurried up to a frog and asked: "Please, Mr. Frog, can you carry me across the water on your back?"

"I would," replied the frog "but, given who you are, I must refuse. You might sting me as I swim across."

"But why would I do that?" asked the scorpion. "It's not in my best interest to sting you because if I do then you will die and I will drown."

Although the frog understood how dangerous scorpions were, what this otherwise fatal foe said actually made sense. *Perhaps*, thought the frog, *this one time the scorpion will better manage his tail*. So the frog agreed. The scorpion climbed onto his back, and together they cast away across the stream. But just as they reached the middle of the water, the scorpion jerked his tail and stung the frog. Mortally wounded, the frog cried out: "Why did you sting me? Now I will die, and you will drown!"

"I know," replied the scorpion as he sank into the deep water, "But I'm a scorpion. I have to sting you, because it's in my nature."

♦♦♦

The lesson to be learned from the frog and the scorpion is that people reveal themselves when unbearable opportunities or circumstances unfold. Similarly, SEAL training doesn't *create* the ideal candidate or change *who* we are, it just adds to what we're capable of achieving by affording new opportunities to shine. In essence, the instructor staff just chips away at the rough edges to *mold* the trainees' hearts and minds into unrelenting souls who know no bounds. If this specwar rite of passage did actually *create* the person, then there wouldn't be quitters; students would instead just wait to receive their "how-to-make-it-through-BUD/S" recipes from the cadre, and they'd never get to reap the benefits of digging down deep into the depths of passion to *find* their *why*. Being a volunteer is just a title, but it doesn't change who you are at your core. Choice is what determines success or failure, and failure is only determined by where you *choose* to stop. It's that simple. It's all a matter of how strong your purpose and passion drive you and how strong a moral fiber you *choose* to enact. It's also a matter of how your purpose and passion are intertwined. It's a relationship.

Humility in the Teams

As a new guy in the SEAL Teams, you're subjected to embarrassing stuff which I won't go into here. But that's the point. The older, more operationally experienced guys want to see just how serious a new guy takes himself and how much humility he has, because the more pride a person has, the less willing he is to keep his mouth shut and his ears open. In other words, humility and a willingness to learn have always gone hand-in-hand—at least in my experience. Plus, the specwar community needs another arrogant operator like it does an STD.

A new guy who chooses not to play the "reindeer games" (the mind games we play on each other to keep guys humble and to cut tension) because he considers himself too good is typically not a good fit, because there is a sick sense of humor that every special operator knows—and that their spouses don't laugh at—as it serves as a reminder not to be too big for one's britches. Stupidity and wit will defeat worry and tension every time, because the former serves as a stress release as it extracts an individual's internal focus of the unknown and all the anxiety with it, into the *now*. There's a saying that mirrors this mindset that goes like this:

If you are depressed you are living in the past. If you are anxious you are living in the future. If you are at peace you are living in the present.

— Lao Tzu

Without the humility to acknowledge new talent, experience, or knowledge as valuable tools toward one's personal and professional development, personal competency and performance become limited. On the battlefield or in the boardroom, you are there to get results. Period. *Who* comes up with an idea or solution doesn't matter, because everybody is there for the same purpose: to win the *war*—not his or her own individual battle.

Humility is parallel with the notion of service, or the belief that your efforts provide a meaningful value that make a positive difference. The idea of *service* is generally associated with a product or provision that a company offers; something that acts as a competitive advantage because it connotes a value to customers. However, possessing the humbleness to learn is also a mindset, which is the main emphasis here.

The word "humility" comes from the Latin *humus*, meaning "earth," and *humi*, meaning "on the ground," and thus the term "humble leadership" literally means "leading from the ground" or "bottom-up leadership." Being *humble* means admitting that a better solution exists and that you didn't think of it (not literally, but you get the idea). Deferring to those who have the knowledge and experience comes from trust and a clear sense of purpose to become better *as a team*. The only thing that propels or restricts someone from further achievement—or sustained superior performance—is his or her ego, because it precludes *learning*. Winning will not occur without humility because in order to understand pleasure, one must pass through perdition.

The loudest guys in BUD/S were always the first ones to go. There is nothing worse than an over-inflated ego. If your awesomeness is truly abundant, then you don't have to tell anyone how great you are since—apparently—they already know. Actions speak for themselves. In SEAL training, flamboyancy was a surefire way out for two reasons:

1. Nobody wants to work with an asshole (synonymous with egotism), and the SEAL instructors had the biggest say about that. People who always have something to say are just not a good fit in the Teams because they like to draw attention upon themselves, which is not what the SEAL community is about.

2. From my experience, people who need to promote themselves and put others down are typically selfish and lack self-confidence, and so the "natural selection" of BUD/S weeded these people out anyway.

◆◆◆

There is an old Chinese proverb about the meaning of humility and service that depicts the humble mindset:

In the course of his growing up, the young boy became distressed. He approached his father with the question, "Before I determine the type of life I would like to lead, I must know the difference between Chinese heaven and Chinese hell."

After reflecting for a bit, the father replied: "In Chinese hell there is a great banquet, and all are seated at a beautiful stone table. Each person enjoys the best of food and drink. The souls are mostly hungry and want to eat, but their chopsticks are twelve feet long!" The father described Chinese heaven in the same way. Confused, the young boy asked, "So what is the difference?"

The father replied: "In Chinese hell, the souls starve because they try to use the chopsticks to feed themselves. In Chinese heaven, all are sustained because they use those same chopsticks to feed each other."

Similar to Chinese heaven and hell, many companies and teams have the same strategies, similar resources of high performers and strong finances to excel, but they fall short. Why? Because the people—managers, leaders—try to feed themselves. They operate with a "me" instead of a "we" mindset and, as a result, create a Chinese hell for them and their team. Selfishness easily steers clear of the "we" mindset that garners higher performance, and instead fuels the "me" mindset that is—unfortunately—so prevalent today.

There is a toxic attitude that pervades many organizations today, one that has been cultivated since the beginning of time. Some people see relationships as an opportunity to serve themselves, as a sequence of *give* and *take* transactions such that, if the "price" of the exchange isn't high enough, there is no value in it. They see success as *getting* more than *giving*. Their polar opposite counterparts, however, see relationships as a means to serve others because it not only grows others, but also oneself. To lead with humility is to influence in such a way that others aspire to follow you—not because of what you say, but for what you don't say.

Humility is an extremely important value because not many people have it, and success comes from having the *humility* to listen to others, acknowledge outside perspectives, and never be satisfied. It is a constant yearn to become *better*. Improvement only comes from establishing, honing, and constantly working on the fundamentals until you no longer have to think, but just *feel* and *act*. If you want to distinguish yourself from the competition and leave a legacy, then get away from "me" and get into "we."

Intro To Adaptability

The art of life is a constant readjustment to our surroundings.
—Kakuzo Okakura

Trying to wrap your head around uncertainty isn't exactly intuitive. After all, asking your brain to process something it doesn't know and can't understand or infer meaning from is an impossible request. The human mind, you see, can't process uncertainty simply because it can't understand what isn't there. Our brains look for patterns and interconnections because they provide meaning, and will even fill the gap with previously held knowledge if it can't make out what it sees. This explains why we can read sentences with jumbled-up letters that don't make any sense. Try this:

If yuo cna raed thsi yuo'er nromal.

What does it say? The reason this works is because our brains fill the knowledge gap with what it expects to see, pulling from previously held understandings. Even though the above sentence has no meaning, we believe it does because we *put* meaning into it. We place meaning on something that isn't even there. This portion of what we *think* we see (roughly 60 percent) comes from former experiences, schemas, and patterns, but the rest is attributed to previously held context that gets assimilated into categories that attempt to fill the knowledge gap. However, this latter portion is also filled with bias. If you really think about it, the very definition of uncertainty defies categorization. So from a functional perspective, we (our brains) are already setup for failure. We can't truly define that which we do not know, which is where adaptability comes in.

In today's day and age, individuals and organizations can't afford the mindlessness associated with the status quo. They must continually be looking for ways to improve if they want to stay relevant amongst the competition, and that means filling the knowledge gap daily. Employees need to be able to think on their feet, contribute, and create the right workplace that wields the right product.

To stay relevant in today's marketplace takes something that most companies fear yet all experience at some point in their existence if they want to stay competitive: adaptation. Lasting change stems from a willingness to change and keep changing. The forces that drive change never stop; they are always there and always testing the walls of your mental and emotional fortress.

Change isn't a one-time event. There is no single organizational overhaul that allows a company to suddenly be competitive forever. Instead, change is ongoing—a way of life because you are constantly learning.

In the military, adapting to change was just something we did naturally. No two days were ever the same because if we didn't adapt, if we didn't learn from the mistakes of yesterday and apply them to today, then we ran the risk of the enemy changing first and therefore getting one step ahead. The longer this went on, the more obsolete we became. A willingness to change is what allows you to stay relevant in today's world and avoid becoming yesterday's news headline. To adapt is to change and to change is to improve.

I like to compare adaptability to that of a freeway—a huge, California-like, ridiculously wide, eight-lane highway. Whether you're an organizational leader or project manager, you know you must take yourself, and your company or team, from point A to point B along the highway if you want to hit the numbers you need to make stakeholders happy. How you get there is up to you and your own creative ingenuity. You can change lanes, speed up, slow down, or take the next exit, but given the guardrails on either side, you know you must operate within certain constraints and travel in one general direction. Remember, this is a very wide highway so there are pockets of traffic—some faster, others slower—that offer you options, just as in the marketplace.

Here's the opposite situation. You're on a two-lane highway stuck in bumper-to-bumper traffic because construction ahead has backed up everything. There's no way out. No upcoming exits to take for alternate routes. You are stuck in process, rules, and bureaucracy (represented by all the cars ahead of you), and there is nothing you can do about it. There is no room to maneuver (i.e. innovate, adapt, and overcome) because the construction—or infrastructure—slows down progress.

The highway in the first example symbolizes adaptability—the process of pivoting to maximize value. You can restructure, release a new product, conduct an acquisition, you name it—without layers of process bogging down you or any other "driver." The takeaway here is that too much process buries the ability and willingness for people to innovate, change, and adapt.

The point of this metaphorical story is that when you, as the leader, begin to structure your business, consider structuring it for change. Adapt and readapt for purpose to avoid becoming obsolete—that's the only way to stay relevant in today's global environment, and that's what this section is about.

Filling The Gap

You can't build an adaptable organization without adaptable people—and individuals change only when they have to, or when they want to.

—Gary Hamel

Change is constant. Progress isn't. If you don't purposefully look for ways to bridge the gap between relevance and obsolescence, you become another statistic.

Think of it this way. When bullets are flying at you, it doesn't matter in which direction you move, just as long as you *move* elsewhere.

This is the essence of adaptability—finding adaptive solutions that fill the void between certainty and the unexpected, and it is only possible with a strong performance-based foundation that gives you the physical, mental, emotional, and spiritual wherewithal *to* move.

To adapt is "to make something suitable for a new use or purpose." Without the four pillars of performance serving as the springboard to adaptability, there's no skill to innovate, no *will* to do so, and no confidence to attempt to navigate the unknown. There's no way to fill the gap.

However, to adapt also requires the awareness to know *when* to adapt. On the battlefield, the acute power of observation is imperative to navigating uncertainty and unlocking opportunities for success. It also provides a comparative analysis for each and every operator as to where he is in relation to not just his team but also the enemy and the environment; he's aware of what's happening at the moment, where his teammates are in relation to the enemy, what each one is doing, and what to correct. It's this power of observation that defines the impetus to *move*.

The four pillars of performance serve as cornerstones to preventing complacency, but that's not all. You can get plenty of rest, feel like God when you give your next presentation, or manage your emotions well under stress but, hey, sometimes shit just happens.

When chaos shows its ugly face, you have two choices: to go with the flow or to swim upstream. Now, I was a Spanish major, so physics is not my strong point. However, by following the path of least resistance you afford yourself new opportunities to excavate along the way that, in turn, afford you the choice to adapt or to continue with the flow. This path mirrors the peaks and valleys metaphorically described in a previous chapter. The balance amongst the four pillars of performance is the source of competence and character that give you the confidence-*to* adapt.

Thermopylae, Greece 480 BC

In 480 BC, the Persian king Xerxes led an attempted invasion to take control of ancient Greece. With forty-six other nations and thirty Persian generals, King Xerxes made his way toward ancient Greece only to be stopped at the pass of Thermopylae. The Spartans, ever so tactically cunning, chose the gates of Thermopylae as a choke point to stifle the king's advancement due the strict confines of the terrain. The pass between mountain and sea cliff was so narrow that only a handful of Persian soldiers could make it through at a time. The Spartans knew this, and would seize the opportunity to pick off the enemy force one by one.

Forty-six nations totaling approximately 100,000 to 150,000 Persian soldiers marched under Xerxes to overtake ancient Greece, only to be held up by 300 hundred Spartans defending the pass.

Greek hoplites arranged themselves into a phalanx, a formation strategically intended to demoralize the enemy and cause them to turn away simply according to the size and perception given by the formation holding its ground. In a phalanx, the hoplite soldiers line up abreast of each other, interlocking their shields so as to create a "human wall." They would march forward toward the enemy adversaries until they got to close range and then increase their pace almost to a run and collide into their opposition, leading them into combat.

The purpose of the phalanx wasn't to kill, but rather to demoralize the enemy into retreat, to hold ground and force the opposing force to turn away in vanquishment.

The strength of the phalanx, however, was only as strong as its weakest member, since any soldier fighting alone had a lesser chance of survival compared to the collective efforts of his brethren. Standing abreast of each other, hoplites covered their teammates beside them with their own shields to fill any gaps in exposed flesh.

At Thermopylae, wave after wave of the Persian army moved forward, and the phalanx slayed enemy soldier after soldier to the point that the body count became uncountable.

Onward the Persians pushed, and even though they outnumbered the Greeks, no matter how hard they tried the Greek phalanx did not cede, the ground growing slippery with blood, bile, and waste from the Thermopylae killing field.

Three hundred Spartans and their allies managed to hold off the Persian invaders for seven days, and they did so by working together synergistically, as one complete system, out of a single shared commitment.

How They Did It

How do three hundred individuals stave off a far superior force of seventy thousand–plus *outside* of Hollywood? How does one overcome the fear, adrenaline, excitement, and chaos of the day and manage to not only preserve himself, but also his teammates beside him?

He adapts, and he fills the gap. To adapt is to assume change in such a way that one's actions enhance survivability. A successful adaptation is based upon three criteria:

1. Preserving the skills that dictate survival

2. Removing or modifying the skills that no longer contribute to survival

3. Reprogramming or rearranging new skills to flourish and win

In Spartan terms, this means filling the gap of the guy next to him. It means submitting to the purpose of the moment and placing all worry, stress, and concern to the wayside out of a mutual desire to win. At the moment of adaptation, a Spartan is balanced among the four pillars of performance and ready to move ahead—where "moving" means "changing."

There are gaps to fill in every performance-driven aspect of life—gaps in one's courage, decision-making, self-confidence, collaboration, habits, team functionality, the list goes on. At work, when somebody takes out the trash without being asked to do so, he is filling the gap for the person who normally does. When you help your spouse carry in groceries from the car, you're filling the gap of time that it would take your spouse do so on his or her own. When you take the time to give directions to somebody on the street, or help your son with math homework, or watch your daughter's recital, you're filling the gaps of uncertainty that exist in their world with the certainty that exists in yours, thus bringing you both closer toward certitude.

◆◆◆

What does this mean for business? How often do employees at the director level, for instance, make the jump from director to vice president without ever getting the memo on how to lead? The unstated assumption is that one day you're a director and the next day you're a VP armed with enough know-how and experience to know how to lead others. The promotion requires that the former director immediately become capable of making the jump from a micro-macro view of the organization to a senior leadership position where a macro-only level perspective is required, but this isn't likely. There's always a learning curve when assuming anything new which necessitates adaptability.

All in all, the pace of business today is constantly changing, and if you don't address the small fissures before they evolve into larger gaps, you run the risk of playing catch up, and that's a precursor to losing. So, how do you stay relevant?

Filling The Organizational Gap

Just as the hoplites centuries ago protected one another from complacency and chaos through continual self-renewal, business entities of today must do the same if they want to avoid becoming obsolete.

Take the typical business hierarchy, for instance. What looks neat and clean on a company org chart isn't actually how the company runs. Relationships aren't linear, but networked. Hierarchy, therefore, is outdated. The age-old system originally designed by the military and adopted by corporate America to enhance efficiency during the industrial revolution has been rendered obsolete for the simple fact that it promotes irrelevance. Here's why.

The very nature of a hierarchical structure places the decision-makers ("thinkers") at the top and entry-level employees ("doers") at the bottom. Imagine, for instance, a pyramid. Take the pyramid and cut it in half by drawing a horizontal line across its midsection, labeling the top half as "thinkers" and the bottom half as "doers." What you have is a pyramid that mirrors the organizational structure of many businesses today; subordinates who have the front-line context but lack the decision-making power to act, and higher level executives who think they have the same context as the rest of their employees but don't. There is a dividing line between those who do things right and those who do the right things.

But there doesn't have to be.

Now, erase that dividing line. What happens?

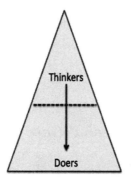 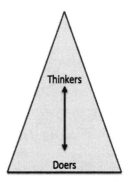

The "thinkers" and "doers" merge into one. They now occupy the same space such that the pyramid becomes holistic and all-encompassing, which now means that people can both think and act autonomously because they all share the same strategic context of what the company's objectives are and why. They filled the gap.

When you fill the gap, you immediately remove the "me" mindset that pervades many cultures and instead create a shared mentality of "we" throughout, because people are now goal-bound rather than process driven.

After spending thirteen years in the Navy as a SEAL and performing over two hundred combat operations, I can't think of a single mission that actually went according to plan. Not one. A new "competitor" always emerged that forced us to quickly learn and adapt to whatever that new challenge was. We began to crave more information and demand it faster and with greater accuracy than before. We learned, though, that it wasn't the information that needed to travel faster but rather our readiness to receive it and our willingness to act on it—our skill and will. Having the right information is never enough. It's what you do with that information that determines victory or defeat. Availability and willingness are inextricably linked.

You see, on a mission, actions don't always run as smoothly as planned. The gap between expectation and reality usually gets filled with the unexpected as Murphy likes to poke his ugly head in. What happens, then, is *more* uncertainty gets injected into the moment that forces each person to question not only their motivation but also their competence. It is here, in this gap between certainty and uncertainty, in between our own readiness and willingness, where the need to navigate—to adapt—lies.

And you know what? Business is no different.

As new competitors emerge, new products are released, and industries change, your organization must be both willing and able to fill the gap if it wants to stay relevant. Otherwise, you run the risk of becoming obsolete.

Take, for instance, the approach of Whole Foods. When the organic food giant enters a new region they don't build a new store from scratch but rather adapt its existing grocery line and repurpose it toward local tastes with an organic spin.

There were times in the SEAL Teams where we conducted missions without any plan. Instead, we just arrived on target, stirred the pot, and viewed the enemy's reaction. It worked because we were in constant communication with each other such that the left hand always knew what the right hand was doing. More importantly, each member knew why (remember the AAR?). Knowing why allowed us to anticipate action. The constant flow of information allowed us to adapt at a moment's notice because everyone shared the same awareness, which allowed each member to make his own decisions about how best to support the mission.

We filled the gap. We covered each other's backside because we *knew* there was a gap, we were *aware* of an upcoming gap in areas where we had observed trends, and we shared an awareness of current gaps. Of course, the most critical part of this equation was that we were able to *perform* and fill that gap.

To fill the gap is to adapt, to plunge into the unknown with little or no guidance, and to come out on top based on the principles outlined in this book. When you adapt for purpose, everyone shares the same intent, so it doesn't matter who the so-called "leader" is just as long as he or she is willing and able to perform the task.

That's what the rest of this book is about.

Adapting to Uncertainty: How Chaos Drives Chaos

At the end of the day, no matter what line of work you are in, you will never reach your full potential if your organization is structured such that your nines and tens [on a one to ten scale with ten being the best] are forced to work for sevens and below. A structure that does this will consistently drive top talent away as they become stifled and uninspired.

—Bill Warner, President, Naval Postgraduate School Foundation

My fourth deployment overseas was to a place that had sprung up as a recent hotbed of insurgency in the Global War on Terror. Anwar al-Masri (AAM) was the primary targeting focus at the time, so everything we did was aimed toward generating another lead toward an AAM capture/ kill mission—but preferably *kill*. As a result, the operational tempo was high. We had missions night after night after night, and at its slowest we had a mission every other day or so. To sustain this operational tempo, it was vital for members to understand why events unfolded as they did so they could *anticipate* enemy behavior thereby building their contextual awareness and more readily willing to adapt if/when that stimulus arose.

We typically returned from missions in the early morning hours while it was still dark, put our gear away, bullshitted around the fire, and went to bed. Some guys would work out, others would go play video games or read. We operated on a "vampire schedule." We slept all day and stayed up all night to leverage the circadian rhythm of the enemy, since nighttime is typically when people are least active, least aware, and therefore most vulnerable.

However, curveballs were always thrown into the mix. If, after going to bed for the day, the Joint Operations Center (JOC) received intel that AAM or another key personality was expected to be in a certain place at a certain time, then we jumped out of our racks, ran to the ready room, donned our gear and grabbed our weapons, and received a quick FRAGO, which was essentially a really quick plan. Sometimes we developed a hasty plan and boarded the helicopters only to have the situation change, which meant our plan had to change. We needed as much information as possible for our own awareness so that we could call an audible if necessary. We could do this—wait until the last minute—because we knew that, at our worst, we could always communicate with each other, move when we had to, and shoot in the right direction. We always knew where the others were, what they were doing, and why.

Always.

Every team member's action supported the behavior of another. Nobody's role was better than that of anybody else, as we relied upon each other's expertise to be effective. It's the same as in any company or organization. There are no individuals, only interactions and competencies between individuals that are interdependently linked across a more expansive network that, systemically, produces the product or service.

The immediate responsiveness with which we operated was only possible because of the shared purpose and physical, mental, and emotional fitness levels to effectuate change. We were organizationally fit enough to perform anywhere at any time.

When you and the team understand the direction you need to travel and why, then everybody implicitly knows how and when to react. Mutual support simply becomes embedded in the process of pursuing a shared purpose.

I did eight deployments overseas while serving in the SEAL Teams, and no training cycle was ever the same nor was any deployment alike. Even before we returned from being overseas, key leaders began to shape our training schedule for the next work cycle. Training requirements and goals were established. Trip leaders were identified (those members who would be accountable for designing the training curriculum, contacting vendors, arranging travel and lodging of all participants, as well as contingency plans). Assets were allocated—or not. When it came time to train, any new threats or enemy tactics, techniques, or procedures (TTPs) that we had not seen from our previous deployment were passed to us from the currently deployed cohorts and injected into our current training cycle so we could stay current with enemy trends. Team members were constantly shifted around, like pawns in a chess game, so as to best accommodate the strategic purpose of the command and maximize organizational fitness. Structure was thus fluid, dynamic, and constantly evolving *with* the chaos so as to mirror enemy trends. Such organizational flexibility thus made our responsiveness—and adaptability—even more effective.

The lesson here is that when you're in chaos and you design structure around purpose, the structure must change as the purpose changes. For us, enemy trends changed frequently, and so our training focus had to change as well. If our mission was to affect the enemy and the enemy's trends changed regularly, then how we went about executing that mission had to change, otherwise our competence would be insufficient. This is the essence of adaptability—and specifically, adapting for purpose. When you adapt for purpose, you create a capable and response-*able* unit that thrives in chaos and is able to work anywhere at any time. SEAL team structure resembles that of an amoeba—it's constantly morphing and adapting to change. What's so interesting is that the absence of structure *was* our structure, as it enabled us the flexibility to operate anywhere at a moment's notice with the minimum viable resources to be successful.

Too much rigidity is the same as slapping the handcuffs on your people. It impedes decision-makers from doing their jobs, hinders them from learning and adapting, and, as a result, slows down progress at the "ground" level. Imaginary walls are erected that prevent members from seeing the outcomes of information updates because they're working in a silo. When people don't receive the information they need, the tendency is to go off of the last known fact, make things up, or do nothing.

As you can see, having a clear purpose, the passion to pursue it, and the skill and will to do so are critical to success. We found success on the battlefield because we knew:

1. What our mission was and why. These two elements— *what* and *why*—are perhaps the two most fundamental elements of execution. When your people understand what the mission is and why it's important, you allow them the freedom of action *to* act because they don't have to run every little request through you, their leader. Instead, employees are *empowered* to get the job done because the left and right organizational boundaries are clearly established—they just need to stay within them.

2. The positions and actions of each team member. Having the boundaries identified are no good unless you know what others are doing and when. It would be akin to the Army and Marines targeting the same objective without knowledge of each other's presence.

3. The likely and unlikely enemy locations and courses of action. This only comes from a thorough understanding of the battlefield (or industry). The more context you have, the faster you'll be able to *move* (i.e. adapt) when the time comes.

The above three points help shape the environment, but none more than consistent communication.

Across my thirteen years in the Navy, every target was different in its own right, had its own personality, offered a different environment and terrain, and therefore had a different "feel" to it. Some were the type that you read (or write) about while others were incredibly boring; a few that were relatively easy to execute while others had a level of suck higher than anything voluntary should rightly possess. We performed missions that Hollywood cannot fathom and that the public will never know about, and to be successful, we had to adjust our physical/mental/emotional "throttle controls" to apply the right amount of force at the right moment in the right circumstance. For instance, you are not going to call in an airstrike on somebody who just refuses to put his hands up because it would be complete overkill, akin to carving a Thanksgiving turkey with a chainsaw.

Throughout the years of facing and overcoming chaos, we would not have succeeded anywhere if it weren't for the right people. The purpose, meaning, and reputation of the team or organization all rest on one thing, and that is the people who do their part that builds the collective capabilities—the *fitness*—of the organization.

To work in chaos, one must be comfortable working chaotically. Whether as a SEAL, executive, analyst, or manager, when you are given a problem, it is expected that you solve it because that is the purpose that serves the company. Overseas, for example, our operational boundaries were wide, but our focus was narrow: to capture or kill a known threat. The means by which we arrived at that end-state was up to our imagination, so our responsibility as SEALs was to identify the most effective means possible to achieve this purpose according to the disparate resources available.

However, operating in chaos is a double-edged sword. On one side, there exists the *unknown factor* of not knowing how the enemy will respond, which forces you to rely on the collective competence of your team; and on the other side, you have complete creative leeway to devise your own solutions as you see necessary. *You* are the subject matter expert and therefore have the most context because you are there "on the ground." Operating in uncertainty—and prevailing—is what affords teams their competitive advantage because not everybody emerges on the other side. Finding certainty in *un*certainty is what defines us in the SEAL Teams because we know that no matter where we are or whom we are up against, that as long as we can shoot, move, and communicate *together* we will emerge victorious. Creative thinking is integral to mission success—on and off the battlefield.

Nothing is cut and dry or black and white. There are shades of gray in everything we do, which necessitates fluidity of thought and action. It is simply not possible to adhere to a rigid team structure, deliberately planned tactics, or even rank when you work in an environment that constantly demands adaptation; similar to how a quarterback calls an audible when the defense changes. As mentioned before, shared purpose is what enables you to adapt to whatever formation, structure, or arrangement best fits (i.e. suits) your purpose, as the next vignette will show.

Baquba, Iraq, October 2007

The palm groves in Diyala province, Iraq, offered a sanctuary for insurgents. The high trees and densely thick vegetation not only offered some unexpected vegetation from a country known as a "sandbox," but they also allowed the enemy a safe haven to hide from our intelligence collecting air assets overhead.

Prior to deployment, we had been in constant communication with our cohorts in Iraq by reading their after-action reports from past and current objectives and reviewing their lessons learned in order to stay current on knowledge, tactics, and enemy trends. One episode from those AARs stuck out in everyone's mind, and it was the night in the palm groves where our cohorts had killed a *ton* of insurgents hiding out, and we were all chomping at the bit for a chance to face a similar situation. Little did we know that our chance was coming.

The push to Diyala province was an initiative to pursue terrorists in their own backyard and bring the fight to them. After rotating into country and slapping "high fives" with our command counterparts, it was our turn to play. Our predecessors had spent three months in Wild West country and prosecuted close to fifty targets, a pretty solid op tempo when all the objectives were considered "juicy."

After being there for about a month—and, in my case, getting shot two weeks after we arrived—we had probably executed close to thirty targets. Living conditions were simple at best. We had built everything from the ground up, including a "prison gym" that consisted of a heavy bag, kettlebells, and a two-by-four for pull-ups. Nonetheless, we were having a blast (no pun intended) because we were doing things that we all volunteered to do.

We went out one night in an area that bordered the palm groves. Two buildings, about one kilometer apart from each other, were known safe houses that local insurgents were believed to occupy. We split the two buildings between two teams; one team would go to the first while the other would take down the second.

Approaching any target is nerve-racking as hell—and incredibly addicting. Uncertainty looms in every corner, every shadow. Dogs bark as if it is their last dying cry and they want to be heard by the whole world. *Will someone wake up? Will someone hear these damn dogs barking, aim a rifle outside their window, and spray us all?* These questions all enter your mind—more so after I got shot the first time simply because the unexpected had become a reality. But you just keep moving and communicating. The craving to operate—to go out, wreak havoc, and fulfill your purpose and passion with your teammates—is stronger than anything else I have ever known. It explains why teammates return to "the game" after suffering near-fatal injuries, why they are *pulled* back into the fray. There is simply nothing like quietly creeping into somebody's house at night, searching the entire compound, and *then* waking the inhabitants up only for them to be staring up the barrel of an HK416. In Iraq, the inhabitants called us "the men with green eyes" because the only thing they saw when they woke up was the green halo around our night vision goggles. That image in itself proved demoralizing for those insurgents whose ideals didn't quite match up to their will.

As we split forces and moved toward each compound this particular night in Iraq, there was something strange about the village. There was activity. It was almost midnight and people—men—were riding bicycles.

Typically, locals were asleep at midnight—especially with a curfew in place—but the main indicator of suspicious activity was not seeing any children. When village inhabitants hear things, and when there are no kids playing outside, it is most likely for good reason; they hear rumors to avoid *something*, and tonight there were no kids.

The man on the bicycle rode toward the assault force. How much he actually saw of us I do not know (maybe he was just heading in our general direction) as the majority of us remained hidden in darkness, but he must not have seen much because he ran right into three teammates who jumped out of the shadows and yanked him off his bike. He did not bear any weapons, but the fact that he was out was enough to detain him and ask him some questions that could offer valuable insight into the area.

Our team's target produced a dry hole, which meant we found *jack* and *squat*. The other team faced two enemy shooters. Meanwhile, intel updates indicated that three to four military-age males had departed our team's compound and headed toward the palm groves.

Fuckers. "Were they armed?" we asked.

"Couldn't tell," the reply came back. *Great, more uncertainty.*

The fact that one of these characters who fled could be our targeted individual was enough to consider chasing after him. Pursuing an enemy in his backyard where he understands the operating environment is not ideal, but catching him (or them) may provide a valuable tip that could lead us toward AAM.

"Teams, consolidate at building twelve and standby." Our senior enlisted advisor (SEA) and team leaders had to discuss the options, which were simple: we came in here for a mission and that mission was not yet accomplished. We had to go into the palm groves.

"Recce, take it out," came across the radio from the SEA, which was the command for the point element to lead the assault force toward the grove.

The Palm Groves

We had to walk through a maze of buildings and side streets to get to the forest. Everything looked the same—rubble, dirt, barking dogs, and the smell of piss, shit, and burning garbage all mixed together.

As we approached the border of the palm groves, we received further intel updates. The individuals in question who had fled into the grove were lost. The vegetation was too thick for the aircraft overhead to pick them up on thermal or night vision, so we had no idea where they were.

Awesome.

"Let's just saturate the area," one of the team leaders suggested, meaning that we could have the Apaches and AC-130 gunship both lay down as much lead as possible in hopes of killing these suckers since under the current ROEs they represented clear and direct threats to every one of us.

Apparently someone liked that idea because the next thing I heard in my headset was, "Standby for a fire mission—and take some cover, this is gonna be close." That last bit of information was all I needed to know.

The air force combat controller called in a fire mission, during which the helos and gunship subsequently lit up the area with hellfire missiles, 40 mm, and 105 mm rounds. It was quite a spectacle—some of the "shock and awe" that reporters had annoyingly coined for the grand explosions at the beginning of the war.

The helos fired their last hellfire missiles and then had to return to base to refuel. The AC-130 fired off its last 105 mm round but chose to stay longer and pass ground updates to us gathered from their infrared (IR) or thermal sensors. Infrared was not doing much good since the vegetation was so thick, so we had to rely on thermal.

The gunship passed the location of two pax (people) within the palm groves, and marked their positions with IR laser. Apparently the hellfires missed because the pilots were still picking up movement through heat signatures. When we saw the "eye in the sky" mark the enemy's position it told us one thing: where there was one, there are probably more, and we were going to go get them.

"All right," the troop chief came across the radio, "everyone get on line" which was the command for all personnel to stand abreast of each other at a distance that you could still see each other, and face the same direction. After another quick intel dump to the troop about the situation, the SEA gave the order we were all anticipating to hear: "Okay, let's move."

Here we go.

From the moment we stepped off the road and into the palm groves, there was nothing quiet about us. Thirty-some dudes with the smallest guy probably weighing 220 pounds with gear walking through the forest, sounded like just that—thirty some guys walking through the forest. Whoever the enemy was, they knew we were coming. But we had two advantages:

1. We possessed night vision and they didn't, which offered us a tactical advantage since there was almost zero ambient light in the forest.

2. We could communicate with each other, which meant we did not have to duplicate efforts (re-search areas). Despite the low light in the forest, we divided our positions into segments, marking our flanks by IR strobe. If you saw a left and right flank flashing light, for example, you knew there were friendlies in-between.

The aircraft was holding strong on the last known position of the insurgent who was still hiding, but the vegetation was so thick we could not just assume there to be nothing else in between us and him. The pilot may or may not have seen everything. Hell, he may have his night eyes fixated on a goat for all we knew (but not likely). We had to hope for the best, but prepare for the worst.

The assault force was a few hundred meters long from end to end, resembling a snake as it slithered along the earth with its ebb and flow of muscle to propel its movement.

Pfft, pfft, pfft!

Pfft, pfft, pfft, pfft! The first shots suddenly rang out. Suppressors are not exactly quiet like they are in the movies, but they do reduce muzzle flash which prevents "the hunted" from seeing exactly where the hunters' shots come from.

"Waingro," was calmly passed into my ear via the radio headset, which was our proword for outgoing shots. Passing the term *waingro* allowed the team to know that they could relax (relatively speaking) because the shots they heard were outgoing rather than incoming. In other words, we were not receiving enemy fire. This sort of communication offered awareness and certainty in an uncertain situation. When shots were heard without a *waingro* call, then *that* was when you tightened up your grip on the rifle a little more, sunk down in your stance a little lower, and opened your eyes and ears a little wider.

Just then, suppressed shots began to ring out from both flanks and everywhere in between. It was like that pop-up game at Chuck E. Cheese where new heads pop up out of nowhere and you have to swat them down before they retract back into their holes.

Where the hell are they? I was scanning everywhere, back and forth, for the enemy—a subtle movement, a whisper, a startled animal. And then I realized what I had just heard.

Why were there multiple shots? I thought there were just one or two assholes we were chasing in here?

It dawned on me that this entire forest was likely saturated with insurgents. It was probably a meeting place for the who's who of neighborhood insurgency. There could be an entire army in here for all we knew.

I can't see shit, I thought to myself. As we marched through the palm groves it became more apparent to everybody just how crazy this was. The uncertainty that loomed before us was greater than any target I had been on before. We did not know where the enemy was or whom he was with. From intelligence reports we knew that the bad guys were financiers and not suicide bombers, which was good news. The bad news was that intel was accurate only about ninety percent of the time.

Maybe they circled back behind us. Maybe there's an ambush waiting for us. Can they see us? Do they have night vision? Maybe someone is gonna pop out of a punji pit like in the Vietnam movies and impale me with a stick. No, I have body armor on—let's just hope he aims high. It's amazing the thoughts that run through your mind when you are walking the edge of peril. Misery loves company—and humor.

The guy we were after was a pretty big fish, too. Responsible for financing multiple IED attacks against conventional troops, this guy had to go away—permanently. There is nothing more cowardly than planting a bomb to kill innocent people and then running away.

We reached an almost fence-like wall of vegetation about three to four feet high, and interspersed along the wall were mounds of dirt. It was almost like a dividing line within the forest that ran east to west, separating the edge of the forest from the deep pockets of "no return" that seemed to emanate from the darkness therein. As I walked along the fence to find a better way to maneuver over it, I heard another *pfft, pfft, pfft, pfft!* Four more shots rang out, except these were closer. Much closer. The shots came from Badger, one of my teammates, who had discovered a guy hiding behind a mound of dirt about twenty yards ahead of us waiting with an AK. Luckily, Badger found him first. Badger was what I like to call "a badass SEAL." There was not much that slipped by him.

Damn, they're right here! I thought to myself. We did a cursory search of the dead body and found a few items of interest.

Meanwhile, the left flank communicated over the radio that they had killed two more. The tension was building to the point that any step could reveal an insurgent lying in wait. You just did not know.

My team finally reached the area of interest, which was, essentially, a big-ass bush. Our team leader, who I'll call Big Country, decided to break the team into fire teams, which meant myself and two others—including Badger—would flank left and create a vertical axis (like the vertical part of an "L"), while Big Country and two others would hold tight and stay on line facing the threat (the bottom portion of an "L" shape). Badger, myself, and somebody else who I'll call Herr, began to move into position. We snuck around the left of the large bush that was housing our insurgent all while trying to stay as quiet as possible. Being in vegetation that thick without the ability to see and thus only relying on sound is like hearing a sound underwater where you hear the *ping* or *clank* and know something is there, but you don't know exactly where it is coming from.

We were in position. The "L" was formed and Badger, the assistant team leader, passed to Big Country that we were set and ready to move. Our intent was to move through the bush and flush out whoever was hiding in there. Before we moved, however, we would saturate it with grenades just to ensure we were not walking into an ambush. We threw six to seven grenades into that damn bush, and by "we" I mean one member—whom I will call Irish. He must have chucked at least five of them himself. He was grenade happy, and with every new toss came a bigger, brighter new smile. Irish could be happy anywhere and is the most happy-go-lucky guy I know, as well as a great guy at that. It was like we were at the Iraqi carnival and our team had stumbled across the grenade free-for-all pit, where everybody wanted to get his money's worth with a toss.

Boom! Boom! Boom! Between fragmentation and thermobaric hand grenades exploding one after the other, there was still no movement. No screams. No yelps.

They must be dead, I thought to myself. Badger communicated back to Big Country that we were advancing forward, thereby letting him know to expect friendlies in his field of fire. It wasn't long before I realized *why* those grenades did nothing. In fact, it took just two steps.

I stepped with my left foot down and then just as I went to put my right foot down, I saw movement at my feet while simultaneously hearing an "*uhhhh*" from below—a moan that seemed to long for something. Startled, I looked down at where I thought the movement came from and saw what appeared to be a man in a white dress lying on his back. I could not make things out exactly because the ambient light was so low.

There! I saw more movement, except this time the human-like shape was apparent, and this man was either playing possum or waking up from a very vivid dream. Either way, there was no way he was just camping out there in the palm grove. *Everybody in there was bad.*

Oh, you're definitely getting shot, buddy, I remember saying to myself, and I plugged him with about seven rounds of 5.56 brown tip—the stuff that final decisions are made of. After shooting this guy I did a quick scan of the area to ensure that there were no other threats. Satisfied, I motioned to the other two guys to continue advancing. I took about four more steps and then heard another Iraqi voice ask, "*Mohamed? Mohamed?!*" The second *Mohamed* was enough to dial me into where yet another insurgent —right next to the first guy, except I never saw him because of the low illum and the fact that he was wearing an all black dress. I swung my rifle around and pulled the trigger into what I ascertained as him. There was a contrast between the darkness of night and the darkness of his black dress, so that's what I aimed at.

Pfft...click.

My gun malfunctioned.

Oh shit! I could not see what else was around this guy, but I knew he was bad, armed, and not more than six feet away from Herr and me. I didn't know how close he was to pulling a trigger or detonating a suicide vest, or if he even knew my—or worse, my buddy's—exact location. I had two options at this point: transition to my pistol, or try to fix my rifle.

Transitioning to my secondary (pistol) had been ingrained into muscle memory after years of practicing for this very situation; hours and hours of "*sight...slack...squeeze, sight...slack...squeeze...*" (referring to acquiring, firing, and follow-through) repeated over and over and over again, with the focus of the next shot being better than the last. I needed my pistol at this point—*fast!* But, I knew the sig sauer would create a larger footprint for me *and* the team since it had a pressure switch that automatically turned on a white light when the handle was gripped, and illuminating myself or my buddies just wasn't a good idea. Plus, it didn't have a suppressor. These two factors would give the enemy both an audible and visual alert of my location and the team's. *Not* cool.

So I decided to work the jam in my rifle. I passed the proword to Herr that told him my gun was jammed, so he immediately jumped in front of me to place himself between the threat and myself while I worked through the problem. Herr came up next to me and calmly asked, "Where's he at?

I can't see him!" I was sweating profusely while frantically trying to fix the jam in my rifle.

"Finish him off, B!" Badger came across the radio while assessing the area. He just kind of rolled his eyes and shook his head. He was probably thinking to himself, *Fuckin' new guy* because this was only my second deployment with him and the squadron.

Meanwhile, I was sweating like a dog in the sun. *Screw this.* Herr couldn't see this guy as he had no point of reference to begin with, so the insurgent may or may not have had a bead on us and I just could not wait any longer to get my rifle back on line. I slung my rifle to my non-shooting side and transitioned to my pistol. Just like a cowboy from the Wild West that I always dreamed about, I drew my pistol, aimed it over Herr's shoulder (remember he had stepped in-between me and the threat to offer protection since his gun was functioning, because that is what team members do) and my white light shined the area from which this insurgent's worrisome voice hailed.

Ha! I see movement... Gotcha, bitch! I fired about ten 9 mm rounds out of a twenty-capacity magazine into this guy just to make sure he wouldn't limp away and tell his friends—and I probably contributed to Herr's disability rating for veteran's affairs for hearing loss.

That was close, I thought. Within six steps of my initial position, I had found and killed two enemy insurgents who were just lying there in wait. They were both armed but they had not seen us. The forest was *that* thick.

Meanwhile, seven more insurgents had been found and killed within the palm groves from amongst the assault force. One member, who I will call the Angel of Death because he just seemed to find "it" no matter where he went, had an insurgent reach up from the bush and grab his ankle. The Angel turned and fired down on this guy, while *another* body slithered around adjacent to the first, and tried to reach out and touch his dead friend, so the Angel shot him, too. It was getting ridiculous. We were literally walking on top of bad guys. The palm groves, we soon discovered were, not just an enemy retreat, but a sanctuary of insurgency.

Shots rang out throughout the night as more and more insurgents were discovered and put to eternal rest.

At this point, the team leaders knew exactly the sort of risk that the assault force was facing and it was becoming unacceptable. After an insurgent had grabbed the Angel of Death's ankle, the Angel passed over the radio exactly what had happened. Once Big Country heard this, he decided it was enough. He called the troop chief on the radio and *told* him we needed to get the fuck out of there—now! In no uncertain terms, he came across the radio and said, "Alright, fuck this! We're *outta* here!" Not much ambiguity in that message. Big Country called things as they were and if there was any bullshit, he would sift through it—which was why he was such an outstanding team leader.

Daylight was slowly inching its way into the horizon and we were going to lose the tactical advantage. Tommy—the troop chief—listened, and rallied everyone up for exfil.

All in all, we had killed thirteen insurgents that night and detained another thirteen. Strangely enough, the objective occurred Halloween night, which we later creatively dubbed "The Halloween Massacre." What's more, Halloween falls on the thirty-first—which is the number thirteen backward. I know. Weird.

Lessons Learned

There are three important lessons to take away from the Halloween Massacre that can be applied to any organizational setting:

1. Don't be afraid to "call an audible"

2. Communicate, communicate, communicate

3. Listen to your people

Here's how, and let's examine this through the optic of the game of football—the American version. In football, the offense approaches the line of scrimmage before the next play with a plan they believe will garner them an advance. Everyone is on the same mental page until the quarterback makes an audible call—an immediate change in plans—for the offense to change, and he does so because he sees a gap in the defensive line or another opportunity to penetrate the defense that previously didn't exist. It takes guts, a keen awareness of the competitive landscape, and trust in his teammates for the quarterback to make that call, and he needs to communicate it well. In fact, the success (or failure) of that audible is a direct reflection of how well that message is communicated. If the team is playing in front of seventy thousand screaming fans, then hearing that audible call instantly becomes more challenging for the wide receivers at both ends.

From the coach's perspective, while he told the quarterback the play that he wanted the offense to run, he also needs to remain flexible and know when to listen to his quarterback and trust his judgment, because nobody has greater context than the guy (or gal) on the ground.

While the Halloween Massacre had many debrief points, one key point was that we had no plan. Everything we did—formations, movement, and maneuver—was ad hoc, on the fly, and adapted to. Each member understood the big picture—the macro—to include the risks and rewards of what they were about to face, and we listened to each other when the risk became too great. We conjured up a "plan" to move forward together through the palm groves and flush out the enemies hiding within. It was simple. No long drawn out plans and no deliberating. The mission was clear, as was our *why*. We were decisive, risk-oriented, and self-directed. We made things up as the night unfolded because there was nothing else we could plan for, except to stay together and maintain awareness through constant communication. Nobody had any idea what to expect or how to plan for what was about to happen, but we communicated well enough to understand what each and every moving piece was doing. A system only functions as a result of all of its components working together. Constant communication is the key, and it is what builds trust. Trust builds awareness. Awareness identifies commonalities (shared purpose). Shared purpose then creates a coalition to drive results.

So what happens when you face the unknown and don't know what to do? You communicate, because communication offers a degree of certainty; something tangible to focus on; a direction, whether it comes from one single word such as "waingro" or from long, drawn-out intel reports or market updates. Communication allows people to mentally prepare for what's next by creating the short-term goals that afford the opportunity to make something out of nothing.

Structure

Companies, teams, organizations, marriages: they all exist for a purpose (a shared purpose, ideally) which is why the form they take determines the level of output—or effectiveness—they can sustain.

The right organizational fit is a purpose-bound structure that allows employees to use their unique knowledge and make their own decisions according to the mission identified by the CEO or ground force commander. That is, structuring for purpose affords greater freedom of movement—or as I like to call it, *freedom of performance*—and should be based off the team's purpose, people, character, and competence which, in this case, refer to both the employee and the organization as each one entails different physical, moral, and socially acceptable boundaries that define right and wrong and help to guide the organization's mission. This is designing structure from the top-down.

Conversely, shaping a structure from the bottom-up according to the *existing* people, processes, rewards, or structure and trying to *create* a new fit is like trying to hammer that same square peg back into the same round hole. Only this time, the pieces become smashed and *nothing* works. Copy and paste practices do not work for the simple fact that people, teams, and companies all have different personalities—it's the Human Factor. For example, it's easy to believe that what worked for company A and what worked for company B will also work for company A+B, but when you dig deeper you see that the "guts" are different. Purpose and meaning are different. Expectations are different. By using a *copy and paste* approach, what you're really doing is predicting success, which is simply not possible in today's operating environment. Repeating the "best practices" from a previous success is akin to using the same tactics from the last mission no matter the threat level. It's like, *Well, we all made it home safely this time, so let's go ahead and use that same tactic every single time from now on. I don't think the enemy will catch on.* Yeah, right! What is happening is you are choreographing enemy, competitor, or industry response, and by repeating the same plan every time, you're training your people to rely upon yesterday's innovative solution rather than the *process* of innovating. By doing so, they learn dependence, perhaps even independence, but not *inter*dependence. Organizational agility weakens as it becomes less adept and more inept. But, a structure that's organized for purpose eliminates the abovementioned problems right off the bat.

Industries and economic demands fluctuate daily. New technologies seem to arise every other month. In the dynamism of today's global marketplace, knowledge is constantly changing and networks are always expanding which necessitates more autonomy for workers to stay current on their own skillsets without having to ask the boss for permission to learn.

To sustain superior performance, your team must adapt to existing trends not only to stay competitive, but also to *win*. Behavior is modified as needs change. Competitor and market trends, supply and demand, environmental and economic shifts need to be considered holistically to better understand the interdependencies that exist both internally and externally to the organization. To do so, one must identify:

- *Those areas that require an equal amount of give and take*

- *The inputs that determine another's output*

- *The people or departments that operate independently but rely on the performance of another*

These three characteristics cycle between dependence to independence to interdependence, but *as a whole* they contribute to the sustained superior performance of the organization, which is the purpose of any organization.

Summary

Knowledge alone will not suffice without the passion and purpose to move forward, a structure in place that facilitates knowledge transfer, and a culture that adopts a *sharing* perspective—a "we," not "me"—mindset.

Chaos drives chaos. Adversity and challenge pose opportunities to adapt, learn, and *create* your own solution to an evolving situation. The key to success is identifying the purpose that propels the team forward and making sure that everyone sees the big picture so that *each member* can be proactive, stay ahead of the game, and anticipate next moves. This is what allows an agile response.

There are four ways one may react in the face of adversity: fight, flee, freeze, or adapt. *Fighting* may prove futile, as some factors are just too excessive to face head-on, such as a suicide bomber or industry conglomerate. *Fleeing* doesn't solve the problem either, it just guarantees more work and a longer gap that you will have to re-bridge later. *Freezing* in place is only procrastination. *Adapting,* however, allows you to eventually overcome adversity by shaping the situation to your strengths. Fluidity allows you to re-pursue your purpose by any means you see fit, and it only happens with open communication, as the next vignette will attest.

Strategizing Against Chaos

And as water has no constant form, there are in war no constant conditions.

—Sun Tzu

The first thing a SEAL does upon hearing a new directive, a change in direction, or an intel update is share that information with his buddies so that they, too, are armed with the same knowledge and can therefore begin making any necessary shifts in operations or tactics (or at the very least start a brand new rumor to get guys' heads spinning). This process—known as "passing the word"—is very simple, extremely vital, and easy to forget if not proceduralized into organizational culture. See the figure below.

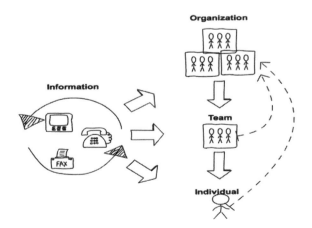

Upon receiving an update, information is shared with the highest level first and then subsequent levels thereafter. This affords senior leaders the chance to understand the situation, justify intent, and chart a course of action.

It's amazing how simple this process is, yet how easy it is to forget. There are myriad reasons why one would not pass the word: priorities change, urgencies arise, someone or something else tugs at his sleeve that says, "Focus on me first!" There's also the innate desire to feel important. Naturally, people want to further their own roles and responsibilities because that's what keeps them relevant; it's what keeps them at the table and "in the game." But in reality, one's relevance changes every day as new demands arise and old ones die out. It's easy to become wedded to a particular idea or plan out of emotional attachment, and there's a tendency to believe that if the idea changes, then so does one's job relevance. If this is true, then the only failure is the *individual's* failure to adapt.

This chapter will highlight how we, SOF, communicate a critical plan in the heat of battle, under fire, and adapt and overcome—and, more importantly, why it works. The secret, as you will see, is a myriad of communication modalities that resonate with each team member on multiple levels. Without communication, there is no Team.

Baquba, Iraq, December 2007

The helicopter landed about a half mile away from the target—or so we planned. From satellite imagery the walk from the helicopter landing zone to the objective looked to be about eight hundred meters. But when we landed, things changed. The vegetation was pretty thick, so after all the zigs and zags around bushes and trees it was probably closer to twelve hundred meters. Landing this close to an al-Qaeda safe house is not ideal but given the circumstances, it was our best option. Just a few missions prior we had infiltrated this same village only to come across multiple improvised explosive devices (IEDs) laid across dirt roads and paths that people traveled. So, our strategy was to avoid those IED-laden pathways and walk the least amount possible.

The enemies we were targeting were bomb facilitators. They cowardly constructed IEDs to kill innocent people—including their own countrymen and women—for no reason other than pure savagery. I never understood why someone would want to kill his or her own people; people who possessed a (seemingly) similar ideology who, through distant connections, may be friends with a relative, a neighbor, a teacher. However, after dealing with these sorts of people over the years I have come to discover that what Alfred (the butler played by Michael Caine in *Batman: The Dark Knight Rises*) said was spot on: "Some people just want to watch the world burn."

Our strategy to win the fight this night was simple. We were not going to try and sneak into this house for the simple fact of whom the enemy was and the risk to force they posed. The danger was too great considering the potential for suicide vests and booby traps, so instead we decided to make them come to us. How we were going to do that remained unforeseen, so our plan was to get on target, stir the pot, and see what happened. We would then create a plan from there.

I know, not a very detailed plan. But that's the point—it doesn't have to be. A strategy to ebb and flow with the threat allowed us to remain flexible by constantly adapting for purpose. More importantly, though, we were able to adapt to the situation because we regularly communicated. What "wrong" would have looked like, in this case, would have been assigned or preplanned positions for each member to assume based on...what? The only information we had was that five to six insurgents were holed up in a house and they likely had bombs and suicide vests. You cannot pre-plan something when that "something" is unidentified and, at the same time, you also cannot wait for the situation to develop because of the threat being posed by the enemy. Our strategy was to adapt and respond to the unknown, which—in writing this—seems completely ridiculous. But it worked, and it always worked for four reasons: the confidence (character) of every man on the ground, the competence to carry out his part of the mission, the constant flow of information, and the humility to respect the enemy. The second you lose respect for your opponent is the moment you become the first loser.

We positioned ourselves accordingly behind a six-foot wall that divided the house and the neighboring area from the road. Every member had his gun aimed at a potential threat: a door, a window, any nook and cranny from which the enemy could lob a grenade or poke an AK-47 barrel out and spray us all. We knew from intel reports that there were approximately half a dozen males inside, so our interpreter attempted to call them out of the house. After a few minutes the first volunteer exited the doorway and walked into the courtyard. He sauntered about ten feet from the doorstep just to see what was going on and then quickly turned around and ran back inside.

Uh-oh. This was not a good sign.

We hadn't conducted too many call-outs at this point but I was pretty sure that an enemy who saw us, turned around, and ran back into the house was not a good thing—for them.

Of course, we weren't about to go chasing after him either, so we had to adapt our strategy. We would give him one more opportunity to exit peacefully but after that it would be a different game. Escalation of force is a mental throttle control switch that an operator uses to match the current threat and then raise the enemy by one—similar to playing poker but with higher stakes. But what happened next would forever shape my perspective of the fight that we—as a team and as a country—were battling.

A male reemerged in the doorway, except this time with a jacket covering his body. Actually, he didn't just present himself again, he *ran* toward us at an all out sprint, only to (luckily) trip over something in the courtyard and fall face first. The distance between us and the house was about twenty-five meters, which was just enough distance for one team member to put all this context together in the flash of a second and make a very important radio call: "s-vest."

We immediately ducked our heads behind the wall, and in the next fraction of a second the insurgent in the courtyard detonated his suicide vest with a loud and thunderous *KA-BOOOOOM!*

And then all hell broke loose.

Bap-bap-bap-bap-bap-bap-bap!

Pfft! Pfft! Pfft! Pfft!

Multiple barricaded shooters inside the house began to engage us with automatic weapons. We matched and raised them two, by calling in Little Birds with hellfire missiles and mini-guns, then following up with an AC-130 gunship dropping 40 mm after the Little Birds went dry.

While we returned fire from both the air and the ground, we communicated our new plan quickly over the radio to get the hell out of there. We peeled right by twos, which was vernacular for two people to get up and move while the rest of the team laid down cover fire. We eventually got ourselves far enough away from the target area to reconsolidate the force, recollect what the hell just happened, and then call in a JDAM to drop that fucking building and everybody in it.

Strategy

There are two purposes that a sound strategy serves:

1. As an operating manual that outlines organizational boundaries and helps guide decision-making

2. To offer a unique identity to its members and thus create a greater sense of belonging—in other words, a culture of creativity makes creative strategies more acceptable

Without the right guidelines, leaders run the risk of having the right people in the wrong places or the wrong people in key positions, which only prevents them from seeing the effects of new modifications as they no longer receive the input needed to make sound decisions.

Strategy is the operating manual for any organization, the blueprints from which a solid structure is built just like a house or building needs a solid foundation upon which to exist *indefinitely*. There are three different ways to communicate a new plan or strategy in order to sustain superior performance:

1. Design for *purpose*—Identify the driving force that propels your organization forward, the purpose that creates value for customers, and then design top-down from there. Trying to design bottom-up with processes or existing structure in place is like trying to fit a square peg in a round hole. It may eventually fit, but the end-state won't look pretty because management didn't get the memo that the new pieces (roles, skill sets, duties) are different shapes than the preexisting ones. Strategy comes from the top down. Refinement

comes from the bottom up. Once you have designed for purpose, your next focus should be on:

2. *People*—The SOF focus on human capital is what puts the *extra* into that bit of *ordinary* and bridges the gap between *excellent* and *elite*. We—the SOF community—take in mere "mortals," chip away the rough edges, and shape them into something that doesn't believe in mortality but at the same time understands unnecessary risk—a unique blend of character, competence, and humility. Additionally, special operators keep returning to the Pack because of *who* they are and *whom* they have for support—a concept not native to SOF but rather applicable everywhere. When you have like-minded people who share the same purpose and "fit" together socially and culturally, the next step is to get everybody on the same page and share that awareness. You do this through:

3. *Processes*—Meetings can actually produce effective results as long as people know the mission and their roles and responsibilities. The key is to focus on what only *you* can affect.

Here's how it works. Imagine your company as a blanket with each and every tiny piece of fabric representing an aspect of the organization, such as marketing, sales, HR, office politics. In addition to the internally woven pieces, there are also external influences that comprise the blanket, such as the economy, suppliers, customers, competitors. Every single piece of fabric is interwoven with another, and another, and another, such that if one piece moves it affects the whole blanket—and now there's a gaping whole.

When you adapt for purpose you don't necessarily change your mission but rather repurpose the organization's efforts to focus on that one piece of cloth that disrupts the rest. The processes in place are what govern the people's behavior and set the organization up for success so that it *is fit* to adapt for purpose. In the SEAL Teams, our processes were the rules of engagement, the standard operating procedures (SOP) and tactics-techniques-procedures (TTPs) of both the enemy and ourselves. But it was the people who allowed this to happen because they possessed the individual "skill" sets of character, competence, purpose, and passion, to do so. Our purpose in the Teams was to capture/kill known insurgents, and we did that through the people and resources (i.e. processes) that defined our unique mission.

You can't control somebody who would rather die than surrender. Such was the enemy we were facing and they were an incredibly difficult force to face because no tactic, no weapon, no incentive will ever compel a man to sway from his ideals when his ideals are stronger than all your weapons combined. Objective Peaches, as I'll call the mission above, is a prime example of how strategic design—and therefore structure—is constantly in flux. All the analysis in the world could not have prepared us for such an unrelenting enemy. How do you stop someone who is willing to kill himself just to kill you? Performing a detailed analysis can help understand their potential capabilities, but not their intentions or reactions. That is where adaptability plays in.

A strategy offers direction and purpose that conveys the need for mission readiness, or organizational fitness; it communicates how the team or company will create value to win their battle and thus differentiate themselves from the enemy or competitors. A strategy is not a rulebook with boxes to "check off," but rather a guide to loosely interpret and write new pages in as you move forward.

Leveraging our strengths and minimizing our weaknesses created a successful strategy for Objective Peaches. Weakness in this case—as in any situation—was a lack of information. Not having information forces oneself and one's team into a reactive versus proactive posture, but we became proactive through the element of surprise. We did not know what the enemy's reaction was going to be, how many weapons they had, or how noncompliant they would turn out, and we sure as hell weren't anticipating a suicide bomber. Fortunately, there were ways to combat this ignorance. We turned our lack of knowledge into a strategic advantage by planning for immediate reaction through constant awareness, communication, and by incorporating the following three strengths:

1. *Collective knowledge.* By assimilating the shared experiences of team leaders and key members and then communicating that knowledge to the team, each individual member could build greater context and awareness that allowed him to make more accurate decisions. Although nobody had faced a suicide bomber before, we all understood the danger of the situation given the village's history (previously found IEDs, known insurgent activity). More importantly, team leaders communicated *why* we chose one tactic over another (bring the enemy to us rather than us sneak in to find him). Our team leaders

knew that problems tend to arise when a mission or purpose lacked clarity, because when people don't understand why they're performing a given task or how their job contributes to success, then they reason independently. In other words, without the right optic (i.e. information), people tend to create their own reality. Moreover, it was the simple radio transmission of "s-vest" that saved some lives, too. This came not from a team leader, but from a member who was heads up enough to see the events that were unfolding, draw context from them, and pass the word to the rest of the team.

2. *Limited alternatives.* There were three ways in which we could conduct this mission. Of these three, two of them were viable but only one was realistic based on our knowledge of the area and the enemy. Such a thorough understanding made it easy to decide upon a call-out approach for the enemy rather than a typical target assault. *A thorough understanding of the environment is key to winning any battle, whether it be on the battlefield or in the boardroom.*

3. *Fluidity.* A strategy that focuses on responsiveness and adaptability allows the force to morph into an organizational amoeba and go with the flow of the market—or enemy situation—as surprises emerge,

while still keeping your eye on the end-state. Our strategy for any objective is to *coordinate* rather than *control* the elements, since the latter is simply out of one's scope of influence. Coordination also implies forward progress, whereas *control* sometimes connotes a stalemate until all the right pieces are assembled in the right order. It is through *coordination* that one's focus falls on the process of *winning*, which is only possible through the rapid sharing of information.

Trying to assemble twenty-five different parts that are moving in twenty-five different directions at the same time is not for the faint of mind, and the *only* remedy that helps maintain your sanity is the speed at which information travels. Every delay along the information highway creates an even longer wait-time at the end, similar to how a carpenter's initial measurement for a wood cut, for instance, must be exact. Otherwise, if the initial measurement is off by just one-sixteenth of an inch, it turns into a half-inch gap down the road and he has to start over. To coordinate the individual movements of each team member with the air assets overhead, our time on target, contingency plans, with the unexpected course of events, we use every technological means available to pass the word. Information feeds the senses and offers greater situational awareness (SA) about the task at hand. Of course, it's not just having the *right information* that enables results, but rather what one does *with* that information at the right time that creates the opportunity for superior performance, and the only way for a group of individuals to become *em*boldened to act is through sharing knowledge. Information allows you to have not only the right context on which to base your decisions, but myriad other perspectives that share the same purpose. Sharing information allows *the team* to anticipate patterns before they emerge, and get the jump on the enemy before he does on you.

Personal Fluidity

Consider, for a moment, how the aforementioned concept of fluidity and designing for purpose applies to your everyday life. When you focus on the journey of how to get "there"—wherever *there* may be—you find that the destination is not what you expected—sometimes better and oftentimes worse. I believe there are three types of people in this world when it comes to finding purpose: ticket-punchers, dollar-hoarders, and purpose-minded. *Ticket-punchers* have little to zero passion and are generally unfulfilled. They contribute hours at work and nothing more for myriad reasons: they're at an emotional crossroads, they're unsure what they want to do, or they're disgruntled with a boss. *Dollar-hoarders* live—not work—to earn money. The goal for dollar-hoarders is to work as many hours and earn as much money as possible such that one day, he or she can live the life they *really* want. But what does that mean for every day life? That is, why do dollar-hoarders choose to put off the satisfaction of personal happiness and fulfillment until later in life? The *purpose-minded* can answer this question, because they are the ones who understand the meaning of the role they pursue; they choose to serve a cause greater than themselves and leave the world a little better than when they found it because they are perpetual learners. Purpose-minded people don't overly focus on the end-state because they enjoy the process. However, this is not to say that he or she will be happy in New York with a map of Los Angeles. They must have identifiable boundaries that help them stay on track for when their direction of travel becomes skewed—and it will. Everyone falls off the wagon at some point.

Our strategy that night in Iraq guided the decision-making that helped position each team member in the right place and allowed us to capitalize on *and create* opportunities as the unexpected began to unfold. In a world of constant change, the only acceptable strategy for success is to change with it—together. The gap between action and reaction gets smaller and smaller every day with technological advancements and greater networking, so the practices and processes that propelled you forward in the past will soon become obsolete. You can no longer "plan your dive and dive your plan" because plans and terrain change regularly. There is less predictability and less time to respond to competitor threats, and so what the organizational blueprints were yesterday may need an "addition" built on today. Where will you or your organization be in ten, twenty, or thirty years when technology not only advances, but *completely* changes?

During the mission planning process, we could have *what if*'d ourselves to death by posing questions of possible scenarios all night long, only to throw the answers to the wayside once we arrived on target. The reality was that that anything could happen if a child saw us, a mother looked out her window, or a single shot rang out. The night always unfolded with the situation, which necessitated awareness and flexibility. Having the organizational agility to respond was therefore crucial to coordinating chaos.

The Enemy's Strategy

Now, let's compare our strategy to that of the enemy. From what we gathered after the suicide bombing incident, once that initial male ran back inside he probably told the rest of his buddies this: "Hey, there are Americans out there and they're going to kick our asses." He then pointed to the most junior member and said, "New guy, you go put on that s-vest I made, and blow yourself up after you run out. Once you kill yourself, that will be the signal for the rest of us to initiate fire so we can all save ourselves." Their plan of attack offered a minimum likelihood of survival. But, the one ace-in-the-hole that the enemy did have was the element of surprise, which was the only component that threw us for a whirl at the onset. Interesting how their element of surprise—or the *unexpected*—was the only influence that stood a chance against our *unplanned* strategy. Chaos drives chaos.

The instant that suicide bomber detonated himself was the moment that our strategy of adaptability began to emerge. The enemy began executing their plan while we had to shift bodies—and fast. Therefore, the speed with which we communicated and the ability to move and morph into a resilient structure was what allowed us to get the "win." The need for *organizational agility* is crucial to any business' capacity to deliver value. But one can only begin to adapt once he or she understands the operating environment. A leader must communicate to his or her people the *new* direction in which their organization is heading—and why—in order to give his or her people the context that employees need to make decisions and execute. The speed of communication therefore dictates a timely response to emerging threats. As anybody in any sort of competitive environment already knows, timing is everything, and sometimes poor timing makes communication exponentially more difficult. If it were easy, then there would be no such thing as conflict, questions, receiving the wrong dinner plate, or divorce.

Yes, I said divorce. Consider the typical life path that most people expect to follow: fall in love, marry, have kids, and live happily ever after. This is the *ideal* reality that people want, but it rarely ever happens.

Why?

Because one tiny detail always gets left out...

"*Ever after*" is a long time! Relationships don't just happen, just like successful companies and teams don't just build themselves. It takes intention, focus, direction, hard work, and constant communication to build the chemistry and attraction from the ground up into something interminable. Nobody lives happily ever after without putting in vast amounts of effort in the departments of communication, shared understanding (read: *purpose*), and meaningfulness. It takes focus, humility, and collaboration to cultivate a shared purpose with your partner, team, or organization. But most of all, it requires constantly shared communication.

Central to communication is delivery and intent: what are you trying to communicate, how will you do it, and why? What is the purpose behind the message? The intent behind communication in the SEAL Teams is to ensure that team members know what the mission is. If you're going into harm's way, you had better know the sort of danger you are potentially about to face. I say *potentially* because things change along the way, situations evolve, new threats emerge, and you must be willing and able to adapt to unforeseen circumstances as the last chapter discussed. This is no small undertaking, and doing so necessitates a specific strategy: adaptability.

As the concept of organizational fitness states—at least in this book—it is the ability to create, produce, and sustain executable performance across myriad domains. The "fitness" comes from the individuals themselves who possess the physical, mental, and emotional character and competencies that, when forged together into a team, create an unstoppable force that can operate in any organizational capacity if/when needed.

To *adapt* is to effectively respond to change, to answer the call *differently* from what you once knew. For example, strategy is the company's schematics for how it will perform over time, and so it *must match* the organization's purpose. These blueprints should outline how new applicants are selected, how leaders are chosen, and the values that govern organizational culture.

In the SEALs we were able to adapt to new mission requirements quickly because we understood the linkages between our areas of operation, targeted personalities, and enemy patterns of life; how the information from one target would drive us to another; and why we had to shift focus altogether if new information came up. We could anticipate mission readiness and therefore "competitor" change and responsiveness. We understood the rationale behind each mission, the geographic and bureaucratic boundaries (i.e. rules) in which we needed to operate, and the relationships between all moving parts of the plan simply because we had the metaphorical twenty thousand–foot view of the operating environment with the ability to dive down to one hundred feet when necessary.

Having an aerial, or "macro," level perspective allows you to see the interconnectedness of elements, how they fit into the overall landscape, and why the action of one creates the reaction of another. You see the whole forest rather than just a few trees. The first time I jumped out of a fully functioning airplane, for example, I couldn't tell you what I saw because my eyes were probably closed while screaming like a little girl (or boy). My blinders were on because the only thing I was focused on was pulling that damn ripcord and *not* pissing my pants. But the more I jumped, the more I learned *how to see*. My competence level grew and, as a result, so did my confidence and situational awareness. I could see jumpers below me, the drop zone, traffic, and eventually, I could *communicate* with others in the air. Some of the best advice I received while in the Teams was, "You must understand how the system works so you can manipulate it to your advantage." When you see the vertical, horizontal, and thematic connectedness of elements, you adopt the Marshall Faulk-like field vision that allows you to:

1. Innovate your own tactics because you understand the internal processes and the external boundaries.

And therefore, you…

2. Decrease your reaction time to make a decision. You can beat the enemy to the trigger, deliver a product to market faster, or snatch up promising talent before the competition does.

Key Takeaways

Strategy is fluid and must mirror the current enemy trends. Stepping back to see the entire playing field—by open forums and constant communication—can significantly enhance one's capacity for decision-making as he or she is now more information-ready. Vast amounts of knowledge enable you to adapt faster because you understand the landscape—the right and wrong roads to go down. Communication allows you to navigate through uncertainty.

An Adaptive Environment

If you practice for anything long enough, there comes a point of diminishing returns. Unless you get real world feedback into the quality of your training, you could be just reinforcing mediocrity. In 2006, for example, our SEAL Team had been using a certain type of room clearance technique because it was what we had been using for years. Our definition of improvement was to execute this technique faster and harder than anybody else, until one particular mission (which is still classified) challenged our concept of what we believed "right" to be.

The last thing anybody is going to do when bullets are flying by you from a barricaded shooter inside a room is rush inside to face the enemy. So, while still on target, our clearance technique changed right then and there. We learned that all the training evolutions in the kill house, the timed runs, and the focus on speed—none of it mattered, because we were now playing a different game. The game of warfare had changed. But without being placed in a real-life situation, we would have never experienced the *need* to change.

The smallest changes can have large impacts upon behavior. If the thought of walking over to the closet to get dressed and go for a run early in the morning is too overwhelming, you can sleep in your run clothes and move your running shoes beside your bed so the thought is more palatable upon waking up. Using smaller plates for dinner, unsubscribing from cable television, or downloading your bank's mobile deposit app on your smartphone are very small changes that have enormous implications for behavior and performance. The takeaway is this: change your environment, and you change your behavior. *Fitness* (in the performance sense) is a direct function of the environment in which you operate, work, sleep… everything. If you want to operate optimally, you have to set yourself up to work under optimal conditions.

What does this mean for your place of business? Among all of the differences between individual companies, a constant feature of any corporate structure is one essential building block: the meeting. And meetings are the first step toward creating the setup for optimal performance.

Meeting Architecture

Believe it or not, meetings do serve a purpose and can actually *reduce* the headaches associated with uncertainty. In the many organizations for which I've consulted, I've observed two recurring flaws that hinder meetings' effectiveness: having the wrong people in attendance, which makes progress impossible; and lacking an agenda, thus failing to require accountability from the meeting's attendees. Remember, people need to understand *why* things occur, and how it impacts *them*. The only people who need to be in the room are the ones who serve a purpose in participating by leveraging their subject matter expertise, and, in turn, drive decision-making.

Performance

To maximize the organizational fitness of your company, you want to work smarter and not harder. Below are some examples of working harder—i.e., here's what you don't want to do:

- *Acquire more and more resources as backups for potentialities to arise (i.e. backups for the backups)*

- *Try to outthink the competition, or collaborate on "what if" scenarios to death*

- *Avoid a course of action and continue with the status quo*

- *Defer to what has always worked*

- *Work longer hours and put in more effort*

None of the above is a proactive strategy for success. Rather, each one is *reactionary* in that there is no forward-based thinking set to win. Each bullet point represents a hope to inadvertently "find" success rather than purposely setting the environment for success to unravel.

Conversely, examples of working *smarter* are:

- *Proactively seek out ways to optimize existing processes*

- *Share knowledge across boundaries. To maximize a system, one must first understand it. The wider the knowledge base you have, the sooner you'll be able to see patterns emerge, and act on them before they unravel*

- *Defer to the individual with the greatest understanding of the problem despite rank or authority*

- *Establish a contingency plan in case "right" doesn't work. There should always be a failsafe for everything that offers guidance and direction for people to follow. What you don't want is for people to be standing around scratching their heads after the primary plan fails. Allow them to create a secondary and tertiary plan to which they can immediately adapt.*

- *Have a purpose—a shared purpose—for everything. The greater the awareness throughout the organization, the more alert—and therefore, more agile—your people will be to make decisions.*

The more you invest in routinizing the agenda, the more adaptability and responsiveness you *gain*. When it comes to meetings, predictability actually enables adaptability. The rationale is this: when you know when meetings take place, for instance, and you know who the participants are and what the agenda entails, you have greater wriggle room throughout the day to tend to other matters. The topics you need to address for said meetings are already reserved *for those meetings*, thus enabling you to deal with other issues as they arise throughout the day.

Below are examples of tools we used in the SEAL Teams to help maintain forward momentum, stay aligned, and shoot in the same direction. A brief summary is outlined in the table below.

Meeting Type	Frequency	Level of Participation
• Muster	• Daily	Everyone
• Intel Update	• Weekly	Everyone
• PB4T	• Weekly	Department heads Key leaders
• Troop Chief Meeting	• Quarterly	Key leaders only
• After Action Review	• Evolution dependent • Every mission • Major training events	Everyone
• Strategy Conference	• Semi-annual	Organizational Leaders

Before going into specifics about the purpose behind each meeting, I want to highlight a few key points—assumptions—that hold true no matter what level of participation. These are the unspoken expectations that each member holds and lives up to:

- *Share the agenda. A meeting without an agenda is a meeting without a purpose—much like two teams showing up to play football without the football.*

- *Time is unyielding. That is, everyone has the same amount of time in the day but not everyone has the same amount of tasks. Be brief, be concise, and don't be the guy who likes to hear him- (or her-) self speak. That guy (or gal) sucks, and everybody knows it.*

- *Time is valuable. Therefore, if you want to reward somebody, consider offering him or her more time.*

- *There is no quicker way to decrease morale than to waste people's time.*

- *Set roles and responsibilities. Everyone attending the meeting should have a clear answer for why he or she is there. If it is unclear, find another participant.*

- *Set expectations and hold people accountable. Without accountability for results there will be blatant inattention to results. If you want to keep the ball rolling, people need to know where you stand in relation to their efforts. Similarly, they need to know where they stand and how their efforts are aligned (or not) with your and the company's objectives.*

- *Provide feedback. Learning occurs when you disconfirm that which you previously believed to be right. If nobody speaks up to highlight key learning lessons or share insights, then no learning takes place.*

- *Stay away from the donuts.*

Now, don't get me wrong. There were shenanigans in some meetings because that's just how Team Guys are—always looking for a joke or smart-ass comment. But for overall effectiveness, the above serve as guidelines for the meetings listed below:

Muster

This is the first meeting of the day, and it is basically a "this is what's going on" information dump. At one of my previous commands, we set the time for ten o'clock in the morning because that allowed members to work out, finish any administrative work or requirements from the previous day, or have family time. It was also a time for each member to bring up to the team leader any personal issues or errands he had to manage. For example, at muster we would get the plan for the day, times and places to be, due dates for certain projects, or medical assessments. The whole meeting probably took ten to fifteen minutes. If anything still needed to be resolved from the previous day, then that would be the priority.

Musters allowed for any issues, plans, roles, or responsibilities to be addressed and hashed out. Having clear-cut roles and responsibilities allows a team member to better direct his effort and focus according to the parameters outlined. His performance becomes more specific and, therefore, so do his results.

Structurally speaking, identifying roles and responsibilities also ensures predictability and reliability. By making clear the social architecture of who reports to whom, boundaries help to orient and coordinate employee behavior and harness it toward the purposes of the organization. Clearly defined roles offer protection from the "Hey-can-you-do-this-for-me-real-quick?" question that arises in the hallway or water fountain and detracts from your daily purpose.

Just taking a few minutes to outline a plan for the day with roles and responsibilities saves time later when things get busy. Plus, if communication isn't consistent, then it becomes sporadic, and trust levels lower because consistency (read: *emotional security*) is no longer there. You find yourself jumping through hoops to get yesterday's due-outs finished today since you didn't see your team leader in the hall like you *assumed* you would yesterday. Daily musters offered stability because you knew you would see everybody at the same time each morning, and so maybe that late evening call could wait. Without clear priorities, everything becomes urgent.

Intel update

One day a week we would have our weekly intelligence update first thing in the morning, which was quickly followed by a team-sized meeting to examine the implications of any new developments on us, our training schedule, and our deployment cycle. This offered the opportunity for team members to address the team as a whole since, the majority of the time, everybody was spread to the winds training or deploying. It also allowed for leaders to connect with everyone and answer questions, offer guidance, or listen to bitching and griping.

PB4T

I completely forget what PB4T stands for, but it wasn't anything cool. I dreaded going to them (which really wasn't too often, anyway) because they didn't *seem* to offer anything insightful at the time. But then again, I worked at the operational and tactical levels, so that was where my focus was. For the senior leaders who were more strategic planners, PB4T served a huge purpose because it allowed them to understand how all the moving parts of the team fit into the larger organizational (strategic) puzzle and allowed them to identify a direction. Essentially, PB4T helped align each department so they could work toward the same goal with the same information.

During PB4T, the lead representative from each department met with senior leaders to discuss their current departmental status and the "way ahead." Representatives reported on their top objectives for the day/week/month/quarter/deployment. Each member took no longer than three to five minutes to give his spiel before moving on to the next speaker. Once everyone shared their status report, senior leaders talked about any new intel, key developments, or mission-critical priorities that needed attention, which, in turn, may have reflected new priorities for each department head and shaped our training focus.

Every department head would rattle off a brief update stating the bare essentials:

"Here's where we are…"

"This is what we're doing and why…"

"These are the dates we're looking to start and finish by…"

"These are the people involved…"

"This is the support we need…"

This round robin would circle the table so that everyone understood the team's priorities *as a whole*. If a department head had a statement of work that didn't reflect a priority or something that he couldn't directly impact, then he knew to place it on the back burner and focus on what he *could* impact.

Every week this would be updated from the previous session so that progress could be measured. The senior ranking person was typically the leader, and after hearing the priorities and interests of each department head, the leader could then give people either a green light to proceed, or a clenched fist denoting a "halt" hand signal for those who needed to refocus their training objectives a little more. If any questions or issues surfaced, all the major players were there so they could be worked out immediately. This way, everyone was aligned, had a clear direction, and there was no ambiguity.

Troop Chief Meetings

Troop chiefs are the main drivers behind putting the pieces of the puzzle together and making sure it looks like the picture on the box. They make *the right* things happen. They help carry out the vision or strategy of the senior leaders and are thus responsible for subordinate members. Troop chiefs were the ones who needed to step back and see the big picture, put all the puzzle pieces together in order to effectuate change correctly, and find the right personality and competency fits for the troop that would make them a better *Team.*

Troop chief meetings were a "meeting of the minds" (in which I never participated—go figure), that served as strategic decision-making to result in long-term impacts upon each team member. These meetings would typically occur either once a quarter or if something of immediate attention required collective input from key leaders.

AARs

Discussed in "Filling the Knowledge Gap."

Conferences

Strategy conferences were well above my pay grade, occurred about once a quarter, and were reserved for key leaders. They generally spoke to much larger organizational components, such as the Army, Navy, Air Force, and other governmental agencies so as to share the knowledge gained from the culmination of all the above meetings with each other and map out one large strategic plan.

Six separate types of meetings, each with their own focus and objectives. However, there is a commonality here, between all of these types of meetings, and it's twofold:

1. To reduce duplication of efforts.

2. To mitigate the need of addressing problems as they arise. The less time you spend in the reactive category, the more proactive you will be and the greater impact you will have. A routine establishes a constant forum *to* communicate. Make the routine *routine.*

In a marketplace of constant change, there is no time to waste doing the same task that your colleagues are doing three doors down unbeknownst to you. One must be able to act quickly when the "Bat signal" goes up—in any organization.

Culture of Change = Culture of Learning

Without an established routine, you are constantly putting out fires to *react* instead of *pro*-act. Opportunities to progress, effectuate change, and create value become infrequent because you are constantly addressing knee-jerk reactions. Holding a meeting with no set agenda, no time limit, and no final decision upon adjourning is akin to summing the hourly compensation of every participant and flushing that money down the toilet. There must be a shared purpose upon which employees can (pro-)act and hold each other accountable once the meeting adjourns.

Time is precious. One of the reasons that I left the SEAL teams was because I was just tired. The emotional investment is high and, over time, the returns dwindled. The best metaphor I can offer is that of a burning ferris wheel that never stops. The BS level was starting to rise and if you stay on long enough, you'll just get burned and begin to stink. Add that pretty picture to the stress factor of jumping from eighteen thousand feet at night, ceaseless deployments, getting shot—twice—and it's ten pounds of crap to shove into a five-pound bag. Burnout can cause mistakes, end careers, or, for someone in my career field, it can be fatal. In any working environment, to keep your people feeling fresh and energized you need to respect their time; every minute counts, and meeting agendas must be on time and purposeful—otherwise, people will lose faith in the purpose or production of a meeting. If preplanned meetings aren't held to strategically align each department, then valuable time is wasted passing the word over and over and over.

Contingency Planning and Cheat Sheets

We had cheat sheets for emergencies or anything else that was critical to know. For instance, while we had an Air Force CCT and PJ dedicated to us for their role specific responsibilities, every operator still needed to know how to fulfill their roles if they became a casualty or were no longer capable; somebody always needed to be able to perform a critical job, such as call for close air support, request a medevac, or deliver combat casualty care. If you think about it, the same is true for any organization to run smoothly. There should be a contingency plan in place for every*thing* and every*one,* but not necessarily a step-by-step how-to guide for each. After all, uncertainty *does* arise, which precludes the ability to anticipate everything and promotes the necessity to adapt. Having a general idea of how to react when the unexpected unfolds is better than no mental model at all. To forego contingency planning is to assume the plan will survive first contact with the enemy, and it never does.

Key Takeaway

- *Structure is vital to capitalize not only on people's strengths but also the tools and processes that make output (i.e.*

people) more efficient. Remember from the last chapter that the wrong structure inhibits innovation, creates barriers to communication, and thus precludes organizational growth.

- *Have a consistent rhythm to share awareness of the competitive landscape (i.e. an intel brief), its implications for the company in the near term, and the outlook for the week.*

- *Consistency builds trust and allows the team or company to proactively build measurable momentum rather than waiting for seemingly pointless meetings.*

- *Superior performance is a constant pursuit, and in order to get "there" you need to use the resources of time and information effectively if you want to operationalize a particular strategy and grow the team.*

The Door: Bridging The Gap Between Adaptability And Leadership

Sooner or later, you're going to end up facing *the door*. The door is the last thing that stands between you and the rest of your life; it is what separates you from what you know best and the unknown of what lies on the other side. There could be a barricaded shooter just waiting to ambush you, a family sleeping, a wire rigged to pull the pin on a grenade, or a disgruntled boss about to chew your ass. You don't know. But you do know that you must go through that door.

While facing this gateway into uncertainty, your heart beats through your chest, your body tenses up, your eyes widen to try and see more out of fear for missing the smallest detail that could be the last mistake you ever make. The stress increases as your nerves soak up fear, adrenaline, excitement, and suspense all in one. It's like trying to tame a bottle rocket of emotion and every second that passes, the pressure inside the bottle grows tenfold—along with the addiction for more. It's a strange dichotomy. The uncertainty of what lies behind the door and the certainty needed to face it.

You are in the gap between adaptability and leadership, where the four pillars of performance have brought you *to* the door, and it's now time to make a decision: adapt, lead, and win, or not.

Despite the uncertainty and high risk, I—we—never changed our expectations, no matter how high the threat. No matter what door I faced, even after the second time I was shot, I still expected that the enemy would lose and we would win. We knew that at our worst, we would still be able to shoot, move, and communicate with each other, which served as a seemingly tiny reminder that fueled a much higher purpose.

There is an old saying on the Teams, that "no plan survives first contact with the enemy". How you react to an unexpected change is based on the balance amongst the four pillars of performance relative to your team and your organization's purpose. If you're emotionally distraught or filled to the brim with stress both at the office and at home, your reaction to change will be different from the person who isn't. The latter is more likely to remain cool, calm, and collected while the former would be anything but. To adapt and overcome is only possible through the inextricably linked capacities of performance—adaptability—leadership (or shooting, moving, and communicating), and their relationships *with each other*. If one is broken, it disrupts the balance among the rest. The uncertainty of the moment—of any second—draws you into *creating* the moment and living *in* and *for* the moment, and if you want to reach the *next* moment, you have to find a way to get there—all while an incomparable and seemingly untamable adrenaline rush fuels your curiosity to see what lies behind the next "door."

And if you do not open that door—the purpose that calls your name, the risk that must be assumed in order to find its *certainty*—then those threats will not only remain behind the door, but they will evolve into an unfathomable enemy that snowballs into a much larger, totally overwhelming force that you cannot reconcile alone. The threats will grow, keep killing the innocent (or keep eating away at you just like every other stressor at work), and metastasize in numbers until they become so populous that they become a much more lethal force than anticipated. *This is your competitor*—and sometimes, it looks just like you.

Risk surfaces when you start to open that door amidst creaks, squeaks, groans, and you don't know how much danger lies in wait. *Did I alert anybody? Are they still sleeping?* If you make the decision to not open that door, to avert risk, and adapt to the threat, then the enemy strengthens. You *must* open that door to "clear" the room, render it safe, and beat the You that would rather keep the door closed. This is leadership.

A Decision Point

The door symbolizes the decision points that every leader—every person—must make in one's life and/or career. A bad decision is better than no decision, but no decision is still a decision in itself. If, for some reason, my shooting buddy and I had *not* entered that room in Iraq, then it is quite possible that the insurgent would have waited for us to leave only to gun us all down from behind. The night would have turned into a catastrophe. A leader must understand the competencies of his or her people and be confident in their decision-making to avoid the potential for complacency or chaos to ensue.

In the SEAL Teams, we receive a problem and, with little to zero guidance, are expected to find a solution. Decisions and actions must be quick, efficient, and effective. To make this work, decisions are deferred to the subject matter expert (SME) who knows the subject better than anybody else. Rank has no authority over context when there's a shared purpose that binds people together. It's when that shared purpose doesn't exist that one uses rank to supersede value and impact.

Introduction to Leadership

Our equation is filled with variables that constantly change—the weather, people, different dynamics that we have no control over. If we tried to control them, we would be breaking the rules. It is important that we understand our constraints, understand our limitations, understand the variables that are out there, and then learn how to deal with it. There are certain things that you are not going to be able to control— the emotions your soldiers run into, the problems your soldiers have at home, the complex situation between the Shiites and Sunnis, the cultural barrier, the standoff between Western culture, Christian culture, and Muslim culture. There are certain things that we won't understand because it is a totally different environment... To prepare an officer for this, to prepare anyone for this, you need to just constantly test him, put him in very challenging situations, and allow them to sort of think and act under pressure and stress. That is essentially what you do here. You are given a task and expected to perform... You see the true colors of people because you see a lot of these guys get bent out of shape. You get tired, you get frustrated, you get mad, you start screaming. You are, like, "This is all [messed] up." You understand their frustration. You got to pull yourself back. You got to remain calm. You got to come with, "Okay these are the changes, and this is how we are going to change our plan." You got to be able to think on your feet. You got to be flexible. I can't stress that enough. That has been our success here.

—A US Army second lieutenant in Iraq

One key function that leaders must fulfill is trying to make sense out of situations that don't have any. A brief vignette from the Korean War highlights this phenomenon:

Facing what appeared to be complete peril, a British battalion was wedged in-between enemy soldiers advancing toward their position from the north, and a minefield awaiting them to the south. Their commanding officer had been killed, but one of the soldiers stated that he "knew how to get out of here" and started to walk toward the minefield. As he navigated through the minefield step after delicate step, the rest of the battalion joined in. The result? Everyone survived.

Once the battalion reached a safe haven, the brave soldier's teammates asked, "How'd you know where to go?"

"I didn't," he replied, "but we would've never gotten out of there and you all would've never followed me had I not appeared confident enough to lead the way."

♦♦♦

The above inspirational story demonstrates the essence of filling the gap—specifically, the leadership gap.

The leadership gap exists everywhere, in all facets of life ranging from personal to professional. You don't have to be in a leadership position to lead. Leadership is about genuine self-expression that inspires value in others to act and move toward excellence.

However, leadership wouldn't exist if there weren't gaps to fill; there would be nothing discernible as *leadership* without followership; there would be no value creation without value negation; and there would be no certainty without uncertainty. Just consider the typical company promotion cycle where Matt, a fictional character, is promoted based on the competence he displayed at the time he entered the organization up through promotion boards. This metric for advancement lasts approximately up to the director/VP level. Once Matt arrives at the C-suite, his ability to deliver and execute (i.e. competence) is no longer the metric for success but rather the expectation.

Instead, Matt is now measured on his character and how well he *navigates relationships* to work and achieve results collaboratively. Matt's success now depends less on functional expertise and more on general knowledge. However, he never received the "memo" on how to bridge this promotion gap, what leadership would entail, and how it would differ from his role as a director (or previous one).

Even worse, he wasn't even aware that such a gap existed in the first place. Now, Matt must stay current with not only the tangible skills of his job function (the expectation) but also learn the intangibles such as presence, communication, and focus—pillars of performance—associated with his promotion.

This section will examine how the previous chapters of performance and adaptability serve as the baseline for leadership. More so, we'll see how the four pillars of performance and adaptability enable leadership effectiveness.

No Place For "Me"

With every choice, there is a consequence.

Leadership is about making decisions for others and choices for oneself. It's about being accountable to yourself, your team, and your organization's mission or purpose. It's also about assuming responsibility for when results don't match up with your intent and things go awry.

With choice consequence thus comprising the DNA of leadership, the genetic makeup of leadership then boils down to two competencies:

- *Decision-making*

- *Risk tolerance*

Notice that I didn't say risk taking, as not all decisions entail risk. This is an important observation to make in terms of a leader's roles and responsibilities. Big (read: impactful) decisions are typically reserved for "leaders" because there's an element of risk associated—one that subordinates aren't comfortable making because they don't have the authority, knowledge base, or awareness of the competitive landscape. As a result, leaders get paid the big bucks to see the macro-level view of the industry and, consequently, make tough decisions that impact their people and their organization.

The flip side of a leader's decisions is this: those issues that don't involve such risk tolerance but rather the permission *to* decide, or act. If decisions can be made by an individual of a lower position (in true hierarchical terms) without even passing the leader's desk and cluttering up his or her mindshare, then they should. If, as the leader, you are making tactical decisions that can be made one or two or more levels below you, then you're not leading effectively.

Consequences of a "Me" Mindset

My last deployment was in 2011. Over a three-month time span, we had conducted close to twenty combat operations, of which only about three were really juicy—gunfights, explosions, sneakiness, ninja shit.

There was one mission we did deep in the heart of the mountainous Kunar region—a known insurgent hotbed due to its unforgiving terrain. Ninety-degree cliffs, rock and shale, rivers and streams, and thick vegetation pervade these badlands, which only conceal the savagery that permeates throughout. Kunar, in technical terms, is an absolute *bitch* to work in—but very rewarding.

When you come across somebody in Kunar, you just know they're bad. Nobody of sound moral fiber lives in that region with any sort of positive intent. Kids, women, dogs and cats, they all know *somebody* who is up to no good. Nobody lives high up in the mountains away from their own civilization if they are not running from something.

One night, our assault force inserted via TF-160 with one full troop plus half a squad of Army Rangers into a Kunar valley. The helicopter landing zone (HLZ) was difficult to make out on imagery and proved even more difficult to land, so the pilot hovered about three feet off the deck while all the assaulters jumped out. TF-160 pilots are incredible. They don't get nearly the credit they deserve despite the *extra*ordinary skill it takes to fly large heaps of metal with the precision of a heart surgeon. Immediately upon insert, we received an intercept from enemy radio chatter consisting of two words: *"They're here."*

Game on, I thought. We had to conceal ourselves as best we could because of the hornet's nest we just put ourselves in, not to mention the fact that we were a small force to begin with. To give you an idea of the level of craziness to which we were accustomed, we had spoken with conventional forces prior to the op to deconflict battle space (i.e. avoid fratricide) and we told them how many of us were going into the region. The Army officer was flabbergasted. "What!? Are you kidding me? We don't go in there with anything less than four hundred, and you're only taking thirty?! That's nuts!" But the small numbers—not to mention the mindset of each operator—*was* our strength as it allowed for two things:

1. The flexibility to change on a moment's notice
2. The adaptability to perform the next task well

We ended up clearing multiple objectives that night as well as a gunfight. Finally, it came time to extract, so we found a clearing for the helos to land. Extract is one of the most dangerous phases of the mission simply because the helicopter has to remain stationary for the entire assaulter team to load, which makes the helo—and everyone around it—more susceptible to enemy fire. As we got into position for what we deemed a relatively safe extraction point, we received word from one of the fixed wing aircraft overhead that there were approximately four males in a tree line about two hundred meters southeast of our position. The pilots passed over the radio that the enemy was scurrying around and appeared to have weapons, but it was difficult to tell for sure due to the thick forest vegetation.

"Let's see what they [the enemy] do," one of the assault team leaders suggested. Due to recent civilian casualties, requesting fire missions had been significantly downgraded to troops in contact (TIC) calls only. Typically we were cleared to engage anyone who displayed hostile intent, which was pretty subjective but senior leaders trusted our decision-making authorities based on the character and competence of each operator. Professionalism breeds freedom of judgment, which creates freedom of movement. When it came to involving aircraft, however, there was a little more red tape.

We decided to take a second and consider the situation. "Well, it's four-thirty in the morning. Call to prayer isn't for another hour so there's no reason for anybody to be moving about—except farmers, and that's not farmland. We just cleared seven different objectives, blew a bunch of shit up, and killed seventeen people. The guys down there are hiding in a tree line. We're in Kunar. We've had enemy radio chatter and activity all night, which only boils down to one thing: the guys in that tree line are fucking bad."

We requested a fire mission to drop (hellfire missiles) on the guys maneuvering in the tree line, so we relayed the situation back to headquarters about the threat we faced.

"Find another HLZ," came the reply from the commanding officer (CO) *sitting* back in the joint operations center.

Find another HLZ? Did he really just say that? Does he have any fucking clue about what we just relayed to him? Namely, that we're on a damn cliff, it's four thirty in the am, it took us two hours to move five hundred meters, and every evil soul in the valley knows we're here? Everybody on the ground wondered the same thing. Our CO had a reputation for making decisions without full context; decisions that he could not quite grasp but did so anyways because they would further his status among high-ranking officials. No matter how well we painted the picture that we had just cleared half of this damn valley, killed the majority of the populace, were *still* in bad-guy country *and* there were four males maneuvering around our designated HLZ, he just did not get it.

"Fire mission denied. Find another HLZ," he reasserted.

"We're not fucking moving. Let's make something happen," our ground force commander said to the air force CCT attached to us. The more we moved the more attention we attracted and the more we risked exposure. Activity attracts the eye.

Air combat controllers are responsible for coordinating air assets like F-18s, AC-130 gunships, and helicopters; they call in close air support and tell the pilots where they want the missiles or bullets to go. CCTs are the best in the business at their jobs.

We decided to fire warning shots, which technically were not considered "direct engagement" since the pilot wasn't really firing *at* anybody. However, if the bad guys on the ground received any rounds or aftereffects of the impacts then…well…shit happened.

Bap-bap-bap-bap-bap-bap-bap! The pilot ended up making multiple warning shot runs and, lo and behold, the enemy ceased to exist. The enemy's *weapons*—that the tree line had obscured—lay by their dead bodies, including rocket propelled grenade launchers (RPGs).

The CO was about to make a very grave leadership decision that could have resulted in disaster, simply because he didn't understand the enemy, the operating environment, or want to relinquish authority to the ground force commander for CAS. Moreover, he based his decision on what he *thought* he saw rather than what was actually materializing. His decision was egocentric because he worried more about the potential for civilian fratricide and having to answer to his boss than he did about sending his own men back home in body bags. I *have* escorted my best friend's body back home before, and it is not something that I wish upon anybody.

Leadership is something we all do everyday, and we do it by filling *a* gap—a gap within ourselves; a gap of unanswered fear; a gap that answers a societal need such as a nonprofit; a technology gap that beckons the call for faster Internet service. No matter the gap, there's a decision that goes into filling it, and that decision is made by someone who has the moral courage to act, the emotional fortitude to endure conflict, the spiritual strength to press on in tough times, and the physical capacity to work long hours.

Promotion And Quiet Professionals

Tough decisions require tough leaders. For someone to be promoted into a leadership status, he or she needs to be deemed leadership-worthy by one's peers, subordinates, and superiors. Promotion into a leadership position should be based off the value that he or she has contributed to the organization, how much of a "we" not "me" mentality he has displayed, his willingness to listen and understand others, his purpose for becoming a leader, and the passion that fuels him.

Influential leaders: they're the ones who inspire, they're the ones whom other people of lesser moral fortitude fear because these leaders stand up for something. The influence such leaders generate creates value for others out of genuine expression and purpose. They do not boast. They do not brag. They understand what needs to happen and they do it. They are *quietly* professional. Oftentimes, leadership is the difference that bridges the gap between the untenable and tenable, the impossible and the possible, the *extra* and the ordinary because it offers an *opportunity* for people to learn, flourish, and grow. In other words, quiet professionals do what they say and say what they mean because that's who they are—or at least, what they've become.

Almost anyone can work their way up the organizational ladder and find him or herself in a position of authority over others. The reality, though, is that this doesn't mean much. As most of us know all too well, many leaders in positions of authority use their title to talk *at* people, intimidating or coercing them into doing things. But these leaders do not add value to the organization because their peers or direct reports see them as insecure, inept, or indecisive, and so these "leaders" use their rank, ego, or overbearing personalities to make themselves feel better. It goes without saying that these leaders suck, and with their influence, eventually, so will the company.

A Quiet Professional is someone who stands out by not standing out; someone whose actions speak louder than his words. He is *humble*, and he leads with *humility*. Humility is the one thing that I believe separates leaders in positions of authority from those leaders in positions of influence. Humble leaders are willing to listen to others and to approach a problem in a new light; their humility, with lack of interference from pride and ego, enables them to defer expertise to the person with the most knowledge and experience—the one who knows the subject matter best—rather than the highest-ranking person in the room. Doing so requires not only situational awareness specific to the problem at hand, but also a willingness to embrace new ideas and be open to subordinates.

To be a quiet professional is to be a humble leader, to be a perpetual student of the game, and to lead with purpose. Quiet professionals do not *plan* to impact others, but rather their ability to inspire is a byproduct of their passion and purpose-driven minds.

To *lead* is to be a student of the game, to perpetually learn, unlearn, and relearn, because leadership and followership only exist through coexistence. They are two sides of the same coin, because in order to grow as a person, one must be willing to subjugate oneself to learn *how* to grow— and that entails followership. It takes *action* to step into the unknown *to* learn but it also takes a willingness to embrace the unknown and *react* to uncertainty as it arises. The consequences from these reactions are the bases for learning.

A quiet professional realizes there are infinite possibilities by which a situation can unravel, but does not get lost in the web of complexity. He or she is always ready—physically, mentally, emotionally, and spiritually— to face any forthcoming challenges. Conflict is inevitable, and he knows it. The quiet professional is ready to take a blow to the face—or ego—if doing so benefits the team; he patiently calculates and waits for the right time to pounce upon his competitor in order to maximize opportunity and mitigate risk. Such is the art of being *quiet*—to have what is known in the Teams as "tactical patience."

To have tactical patience is to wait for a situation to develop enough until the right moment presents itself and then "zoom in" only when necessary. Picture an eagle soaring in the sky. He scopes the terrain below from an aperture of one thousand feet above the ground until the moment he sees his prey, and then his focus narrows as he dives down to ground level for the kill. The rise and fall of the eagle, the ebb and flow of the ocean, the give and take in a relationship, are all representative of the spectrum of mental focus and intensity that I call the Mental Throttle Control.

The Mental Throttle Control is a cognitive "gear shift" that allows quiet professionals to speed up, slow down, stop, or end the race—whatever their pursuit might be—but always in at a time of their choosing. By definition then, there is an unspecified amount of "gear shifting" required to win since they do not know how long the proverbial race will be, and it is for this reason that quiet professionals remain *undefined* in their will to win.

Becoming *boundless* means stopping at no ends to achieve your mission. When a SEAL goes out on a mission, he flips a mental switch to the "on" position and assumes a fighting mentality. He makes the mental shift from being a friend, a jokester, or a parent into the role of a fearless, unstoppable warrior with an iron will who stops at no end to protect his buddies and complete his mission. Whatever he does out there in the field is something that he *wants* and *chooses* to do because it provides him meaning and serves a purpose. In doing so, he unlocks the mental and emotional boundaries that afford him the resiliency and determination to win at all costs. Michael Monsoor, when he jumped on an enemy grenade to protect his team, was boundless in his approach to winning; the Extortion 17 flight, full of Navy SEALs who went to rescue Rangers trapped in a gunfight, knew they were flying into a heavy volley of fire, but their mentalities were boundless because they did what they had to do to rescue their brethren.

To the credit of his mental throttle control, he can walk through village after war-torn village filled with carnage until, after passing the last house, he chooses to "shift gears" back into a role of normalcy. He can once again carry out his role of being an everyday person, a father, or a husband, and his warrior self is temporarily quieted as he picks up a newborn child to sing him a lullaby, or hugs his wife that he has so dearly missed. The *boundless* state is not something by which a quiet professional labels himself, but rather a tool he chooses to employ when the situation dictates—when the mental gear shift switches to high, action is called for, it is his time to act, and failure is not an option. It is the power of choice.

Effective leaders engage their mental throttle control to zoom in and out as situations unfold—it is the essence of social and emotional intelligence—because they are confident enough to know that they possess the competence to win. The quiet professional is thus cautious and fearless as the situation develops, cunning in his course of action, and quietly composed while mentally planning his opponent's defeat. Tactically patient people are those who have already run through their minds a planned course of action that results in one thing: *their* win, and the enemy's loss.

Leadership in the Teams

I would be remiss if I did not offer some leadership lessons learned from the Teams—observations of senior leaders who contributed to or stifled success.

There are some amazingly strong leaders in the SEAL Teams. However, there are also some complete turds—disgustingly incompetent pukes that know nothing other than kissing ass and conforming to others' personal biases as their only means of promotion.

The SEAL community is very small—the smallest of all specwar communities in the armed forces—which is both good and bad. Such a small group of people lends itself to more personal interaction—and, thus, a greater focus on reputation. At the same time, the unavoidable bias of groupthink results, which can be detrimental to a person's career if a key leader has a personality conflict or feels threatened by a subordinate who is smarter, more courageous, and willing to speak up and ask, "Why?"

Advancement within the Teams has thus come to weigh heavily on conformism and personal networking rather than professional judgment and competence. There's a tendency—and this goes for corporate America, too—to ignore existing problems and instead sweep them under the rug because it's easier, only for that person to linger around like a bad habit. Promotion should be based on the attributes that the team, organization, or company defines as valuable, such as service, courage, or character.

Performance in one's last job shouldn't matter because you are no longer *in* that job. Promoting within one's own subject matter expertise is a surefire way to reinforce obsolescence. What I mean is, what a person knows in his or her respective field—and what defines his or her reputation—is not indicative of how effective he or she will be as a leader. The practices are not the same, and, therefore, the traits are not the same. The system of selecting a leader based on one's performance as a direct report is obsolete for the simple fact that we have all been around "leaders" who have no (read: *zero*) business having any sort of decision-making power. Advancement should not be the reward for doing what you already knew how to do.

This is just my opinion, but for someone to be promoted into a leadership status, he or she needs to be deemed leadership-worthy by one's peers, subordinates, and superiors. Promotion into a leadership position should be based off the value that he or she has contributed to the organization, how much of a "we" not "me" mentality that person has displayed, his or her willingness to listen and understand others, their purpose for becoming a leader, and the passion that fuels that person.

Leadership should be a *process* rather than a pathway. In other words, if you wait long enough in (almost) any career field, you'll be promoted to a higher position. While you may not achieve the upper echelon of CEO or President, your advancement into the executive level is heavily based on the time you spend in your career field. Don't get me wrong, not all organizations operate this way, but I *know* you can think of specific leaders within your company who are anything but.

Here's the solution. An organizations is an ecosystem of interconnected parts—relationships, departments, personalities, internal and external resources and influences, personal agendas—whose independent initiatives are actually interdependent, as they converge to promote one single purpose: their survival—and hence, *organizational* survival.

Just as a forest in nature is self-governing (i.e. it manages its own survival as a whole due to the internal and external influences that comprise it, such as animals that regulate population, plants that generate oxygen, and sunlight that aids photosynthesis), organizational success can be found *within* the organization. Solutions are found by sharing knowledge such that employees gain insight about other departments and the company as a whole. So, just as a forest relies on itself for survival, look to connect more of your organization to itself if you want to sustain its inevitability. Being connected to people allows us to adapt, as adaptability hinges on relationships and information, as the next chapter will show.

The SEAL Secret Sauce

The Egyptian inquired of the Spartans why they wore their hair long. Olympieus replied, quoting the lawmaker Lykurgus, 'Because no other adornment makes a handsome man more comely or an ugly one more terrifying. And it's free.
—Steven Pressfield, *Gates of Fire*

Grooming and military bearing has never been a SEAL's strong point, which is one of the reasons why we possess such a "cowboy-ish" reputation. Additionally, every member has a healthy disregard for authority, which is pretty ironic considering that every man volunteered for military service. But the second, and more important feature that defines our "cowboy" activity is the creativity that is inculcated into a SEAL's thought process from day one of training and then proliferates into a culture of innovation; a way of work that questions "industry" trends and adapts to the most effective strategy to win. It is something SEALs pride themselves on—this outside-the-box thinking—and is what sets us apart from all other SOF. Because of this willingness to challenge the status quo and question what *is*, we lead ourselves toward alternative solutions that the larger conventional military doesn't understand.

Let's face it. Anybody with the right resourcing, funding, and training can become an "expert" in his or her field. What defines *us* is the lack of structure in our organization, and the minimal amount of "hoops" (i.e. processes) we are required to jump through to get things done. In other words, we live by "big boy rules" that afford just enough space in which to operate and an equal amount to hang oneself.

Big boy rules exist because of the level of professionalism at which members are expected to perform. If you constantly need to be reminded of instructions, meeting times, or purpose for work, then you're the wrong guy for the job. Period. That's not the sort of proactivity that defines a professional. The behaviors that *do* define high-performing individuals (and therefore, organizations), however, are the following:

- *Showing up on time for a meeting*

- *Knowing your job role and responsibilities, how they relate to others', and how they all tie into the mission*

- *Being prepared—always*

- *Asking for clarification when a project is ambiguous*

- *Asking for help you need it*

- *Taking care of personal matters at home and leaving them at home. When you're at work, you work*

- *Making unbiased, rational decisions based on logic rather than using emotion or personal opinion as a basis for judgment*

- *Respecting your coworkers—you don't have to like everything or everybody with whom you work, you just have to work*

Make no doubt about it, SEALs are the furthest component from the military, *in* the military. We are decentralized, autonomous, and agile inside a military that is anything but. Because we are such a small force, both relative to other SOF, the conventional military, and the enemy on the battlefield, there is very little room for error. In fact, there is *zero*. But, in order to effectuate sustained high performance, we must share our knowledge and experience with other SEALs so that *they* can be successful and return home safely.

Every SEAL—not just the officers—is expected to be able to lead—to make the right decisions at the right times that further the team's mission. As a result, individual thinking and innovation is expected to solve difficult problems with limited resources.

The above lifestyle is only understood by those men who live and work in "The Brotherhood," and when this aptitude is combined with both the organizational structure and culture of the SEAL Teams, it makes for an astoundingly effective team. Men are expected to be thoughtful and have the self-discipline to seek constant and never-ending self-improvement. Most importantly, each operator relentlessly pursues a personal and professional endeavor to harness new ways and better approaches to warfare. In other words, he becomes a student of the game.

SEAL operators are constantly questioning, brainstorming, and looking for *a better way*—we must, given the nature of our job. If we stay in one place too long, the enemy discovers us, and the team gets compromised. This line of thinking thus necessitates perpetual learning and improvement to constantly seek out "the next best thing."

How to Create a "Pack-Minded" Culture

Culture is everything. It serves as an organizational brand that attracts or repels future talent. A positive culture can either compel employees to get out of bed in the morning and walk through the rain while being cold, wet, and miserable, or be the decision point to throw in the towel in search of a new, bright, and shiny (career) ball.

In organizational cultures where entitlement, selfishness, and ego are the daily specials on the menu, how can you—as a leader—create the special sauce that turns a "me" culture into a "we" culture? How can you change people's point of focus from the individual level and shift it toward one that considers the overall benefit of the team or company?

Here's how: you add another ingredient. That is, you need to interject the special *team* sauce into *everything* that you—and your people—do.

No Place for "Me"

Remember that old bumper sticker that said, "Mean people suck"? Let me modify that for you: "Me" people suck. At BUD/S, from day one, each SEAL trainee is exposed to a sense of higher purpose—an aspiration to reach beyond himself and focus on what will serve the entire class rather than his own personal need. Trainees quickly learn that selflessness is the foremost metric for personal worth as it immediately shapes one's reputation. In fact, there are three priorities against which SEALs measure selflessness:

The mission.

The team.

The individual.

The mission always comes first, followed by the team that supports the mission, and then the individuals who comprise the team. A shared purpose is what bridges the gap between good and great, mediocrity and superiority. It turns a group of ordinary individuals into an *extraordinary* team of professionals who share the same focus, same mission, same purpose. In essence, there is no "me."

Everything in the SEAL Teams is built around a Team culture. See for yourself:

- *We're called the SEAL Teams. We do everything together. Beginning day one of BUD/S, each student has a "swim buddy" (which is just another student in the class) everywhere he goes. If he needs to take out the trash, he grabs a swim buddy. If nature calls and he has to use the bathroom, he takes a swim buddy. If he has to face a SEAL instructor for punishment, he solicits a very unhappy swim buddy and they both endure punishment together (misery loves company, right?). Everything is done together because that's what a Team is about.*

- *We refer to each other as Team Guys, not "SEALs," not "friends," not "coworkers." It doesn't matter one's age, background, or previous arrest record (hey, it happens!). Everything he does is for the betterment of the Team.*

- *We work in Team Rooms. At each SEAL command exists Team Rooms that house the smaller teams that comprise the larger command. Each room is one large, open, shared space that—by simple design—fosters transparency and inclusion rather than silos and separation. Each Team Room has its own personality depicted by team pictures, memorabilia, quotes, and random wall art that all serve to create the unique identity of the operators within.*

- *We share a Team motto. A common saying among the community is "Teams 'n' shit," which refers to two things that determine our focus:*

1. The Team

2. Everything else

If you want to interject more of a "we" culture, change your focus. As Peter Drucker once said, "what gets measured gets improved." The only way to change behavior at scale is to change the metrics to which people align their efforts. Find reasons for more collective forums. Consult each other in group settings. Get rid of the cubicles (for heaven's sake, *please* get rid of the cubicles!). Refer to each other as teammates. Have team lunches, team forums, team barbecues. There is no secret sauce to newness other than courage and belief.

Here's an example. Let's take creativity. If you want to become more creative, one way to do so is to set a goal of generating five new ideas every day for a month so your mind starts developing the habit of creativity. Similarly, by interjecting a "we" focus into every aspect of the company, people's minds begin to search for that team component, and teamwork becomes the habit; it becomes the priority of focus rather than a nice focus to have.

If you want to build a team culture, you must work, eat, and do things *together*. Only then will your people's mindsets begin to shift away from "me" and more toward "we."

Culture and Climate

An organization's culture reflects the character for which it stands; the behaviors that uphold its principles that garner an "elite" reputation, or the name brand that dwindles away into nothingness. Company culture must coexist with its sibling—climate—as they are both the lifeblood of their organization. A company's culture and climate will either attract and retain high potentials or push away the skill and will that turn *good* companies into *great* organizations. Culture and climate are both the intangible contributors to the bottom line.

Whenever I told people I was in the military I sometimes heard comments such as "I just wouldn't like being told what to do all the time," to which my response was, "Me neither." Unlike the rigid hierarchy portrayed in the movies or passed through public perception, we had enough rope to hang ourselves if we wanted. SEALs are known throughout the special operations community as being extremely creative.

DEVGRU is probably the most unmilitant component of the military. When I first arrived at the Navy's tier one unit, beards and long hair were the norm, uniforms were nonexistent, and we made decisions that "made sense." That is, we ignored the silly, unimportant rules and bullshit that precluded effectiveness because there were more important things to focus on—like going to war—to broaden our expertise. When you train intensely for life or death battles, things like polished boots or a five o'clock shadows on your face just seem inconsequential. It was the aforementioned "big boy rules" that afforded leniency and flexibility when possible but were also constrictive and mandatory under pressure. Of course, how you—as an individual—are perceived is how you are received, which was why the other branches of service considered us "undisciplined cowboys" when in reality, we just had a different culture that they didn't understand.

Rank was insignificant. I didn't realize the rank of other team members until about a year and a half after I arrived into the squadron simply because it didn't matter. We worked on a first name basis. The number of stripes on your sleeve or the amount of brass on your collar had no bearing on who you were as an individual or what you could produce as a professional. It was character and competence—not tenure—that garnered respect.

Culture and climate define the "feeling" of what it means to go into work. I always told myself that the day I did not enjoy getting up and going into work was the day before my last. Once purpose changes and you no longer derive meaning from your efforts, it's time to move on. Without fear, and without regrets. And that's what happened.

Anyways, an organization's culture needs to reflect the processes that are known to create value. Strategy, structure, and people all define company culture—but are not the only things. Culture refers to how work gets done, such as the processes, networks, unwritten rules that govern behavior, and the morale that can propel or hinder progress. Knowledge sharing, open communication, and collaboration are all practices we know to be important, yet not always exemplified—at least not effectively. A Team Room, conversely, was a place where everyone worked together in one large open space. They may be working on a task pertinent to them, but if any news came out or if somebody had a question then that information was openly shared and immediately received. There were no borders that could obstruct the communication flow. Interaction was constant and always playful, which yielded a positive climate. The physical openness thus broadened members' awareness of the structural interdependencies that made up the organization as one complete system. An open environment provided "real time" information for everyone to not only absorb new information, but also get feedback on how the current processes were evolving and to be ready for any changes. Staying in the "information fight" allows you to act before you must react. Trust grew because members could not only see what other teammates were doing, but also hear about others' roles and responsibilities that were openly shared. The inclusivity and constant interaction thus broadened each member's understanding of how things worked and if there was any ambiguity, it was solved right then and there. This was performance optimization.

Climate, culture's younger brother, refers to what it's like to work for someone. Leaders, managers, and cohorts create a climate that embraces positive behavior or multiplies toxic attitudes, just like adding water to a Gremlin.

Both culture and climate convey something special to which you belong, something to which nobody else is privy save the other selectees with whom you've shared a rite of passage. A positive work environment elicits greater effort from people because their passion is ignited, they become hungry to learn and to develop competence and exemplify what the "right" employee looks like. The coworkers with whom you work and share this "feeling" become your family, your support network, and you continually learn and prosper through the humble acknowledgement of perpetual learning, because you *want* to improve upon the other areas of development that you have yet to explore.

The best way to describe the culture of the SEAL Teams is "open." Naval Special Warfare is flatly structured and drives information downward to the most effective level, such that an individual can effectuate change at his or her level. If you are doing the job of somebody one or two or three levels "down" from you, then you are not serving the organization effectively because you're not doing *your* job effectively—you are not leading. You need only focus on what you can effect given your job role and responsibility. When you start working in other people's business, you begin to lose sight of the overall business because there's nobody at the wheel directing the company toward "true north."

There is a drastic difference between how tier-one organizations operate and how organizations in the civilian world get things done. The physical dividing line that separates employees such as cubicles, walls, personal rooms, all contribute to tiny inconveniences that add up to minutes wasted over the course of a day. Getting up and walking to someone's desk takes time, and sending an email to have the same conversation takes time, much like reading that silly email is probably another thirty seconds of your life you will never get back. It's inefficient.

When a major decision or important update is discovered, a business executive typically makes a call, sends out messages to various people, and basically filters his information down the organizational silos in hopes that people will follow. This practice is inefficient for three reasons:

1. It is a duplication of efforts (with regard to emails and phone calls).

2. It is not inclusive.

3. It is not transparent.

Enclosed spaces compartmentalize not just employees, but knowledge. Awareness becomes restricted, funneled. There is no transparency because unless you're in the "email chain" you won't know any details. Thus the perception becomes one that leaders are not being authentic, or that they have something to hide because emails are considered personal and if you're not on the distribution list, well, then there must be a reason!

Creating the Right Climate

The right climate speaks to the organization's purpose. When you walk in a SEAL Team Room, for example, you're taken aback by the sheer size; the room is enormous. Computers line the walls, long tables in the middle. Weapons from past missions serve as reminders of our past as they hang randomly throughout the room—each with its own personalized inscription about what happened on a particular night. A plaque made of brass and infused with our team flag from plastic explosive is *set* into the floor like another piece of tile. Pictures of fallen teammates and their shadow boxes line the wall—higher than anything else in the room—and pictures of teams and teammates, both active and retired, are displayed to remind us all where we (the team) came from. The pictures serve as a reminder that this arena, this "setting," is a family setting; a place where brothers talk openly, argue, fight, laugh, and memorialize. Pictures communicate what is important not only to you, but to the organization. The things important to us are each other. Just as people have pictures of their spouse or kids on their desks, we have pictures of our Team, because that is whom we serve at the end of the day. All the pictures, mementos, sayings, and slogans serve a purpose, which is to remind us of our history, our presence, and the legacy we wish to leave behind.

Have you ever walked into a professional sports team locker room, or a coach's office? If so, you probably saw trophies, quotes from Vince Lombardi or some other iconic figure whose personal values the team espouses, and team pictures because they all create meaning for the players. Everybody needs reminders of who they are, where they are, and what their mission is. This is the process of creating a winning climate: to focus on priorities, values, and expectations.

Change Your Environment, Change Your Performance

The only way to change from *good* to *great* and from *great* to *badass* is to change your environment. Improvement is only attained by breaking through what one "knows" and into experiencing the "unknown." Uncertainty is the only place where *value* is created; for only in the unknown do you actually find your *true* self.

Repeat exposure to the same routine only reinforces impertinence and suppresses creativity. A professional athlete competes against other professionals every week. Yes, his or her learning is constant but after a certain point the learning curve flattens out, and in order to make a giant leap and bridge the gap between one's current physical, mental, and emotional fitness, there has to be something new that creates an "Aha!" moment. Laying out in the sun every day is not going to get you any more tan because your skin is used to that one hour of repeat exposure. In order to turn up the heat, you must lengthen your time in the sun. You need to change the stimulus.

Similarly, to perform "at the next level" one must completely leave his or her circle of physical, mental, and emotional comfort and enter something new entirely; something that will strip away the outer shell at the surface and reveal one's true character *potential*; something that forces oneself to dig deep and discover a whole new meaning of fear, elation, uncertainty, pain, and triumph. In order to understand the value of heaven, one must endure hell. Extreme performance calls for extreme challenges, which yield extremely fruitful rewards.

I once met another former SEAL who dedicated his profession to doing just this. He had just returned from an expedition to South America with a small contingent of professional athletes, from which the athletes returned with a whole new outlook on life. They had trekked through the Andes

Mountains for five days, following a route that not even the guides had walked before. The whole point was to validate the concept of operating in uncertainty. Nobody had worked together before yet they all shared a common bond—even with the cadre since *they* had never trekked these trails before. What the athletes learned as they returned to the United States was that they could do anything—*anything*—that they put their minds to.

Think about that for a second. Is there anything holding you back from pursuing your life's mission? There shouldn't be, because nothing lasts forever.

Nothing.

I believe in something I call "perpetual transience," which refers to a constant state of temporariness; a state in which absolutes do not exist but instead only momentary setbacks that serve as learning opportunities to build and reflect upon on the journey toward self-actualization—knowledge that cultivates the potential for success. The athlete, businessperson, or any other working professional that wants to improve him- or herself must leave the climate and culture to which he or she is accustomed and become immersed in another. Only this sort of dedication and commitment will offer the learning experience that bridges the gap toward new perspectives and experiences—both of which offer greater context for decision making in the future.

Before I went to BUD/S, I didn't truly know what it meant to "push myself." After every conditioning run in BUD/S, I would think to myself, "Gosh, that run really sucked. That was the hardest we ever ran." Then the next day rolled around and *that* conditioning run became the hardest one we ever ran. The mantra of "The only easy day was yesterday," was a no shitter. There were triathletes, collegiate wrestlers, and ISKA karate dorks who all volunteered for SEAL training for the same reason, but they were introduced to another level of performance and expectation, of what it meant to sacrifice and to endure.

It was a whole new level.

It was a brand new experience to which the aforementioned quitters' minds, bodies, and souls were unfamiliar, and they quit because this new experience of hardship was not something their minds could fathom, and it wasn't a culture they chose to accept.

Summary

The Pack is a social bond that catapults you forward when your passion lags. It can be found amongst friends, family, neighbors, co-workers, or the culture of your organization. Belonging to something of a higher purpose, a greater cause, compels you to "do right" when others unnecessarily do *wrong*.

Friends, teammates, and family keep you in check to help you get *there*— wherever "there" may be. We are all products of our culture—personally and professionally. In order to deliver the results that organizations seek, culture must lead the way and exemplify the model that people espouse. Culture and climate are the internal "branding" of your team or company— the way things get done—or not—that are derivative of the strategy, people, and structure that make up the organization's perpetual *learning*. *This* is your strategy. *This* is how you lead.

Leading With "We"

As is your sort of mind, so is your sort of reach; you'll find what you desire.

—Robert Browning

Contrary to everything you've ever been told, knowledge is *not* power. Chaos is what evolves out of the very mindset that the person with the most knowledge—the most "power"—wins. Nowadays, that line of thinking will sink a ship faster than an iceberg on the Titanic.

The days of information hoarding—of only a few "powerful" people at the top of the outdated organizational pyramid holding on to that last bit of data as if *nobody* else could replicate it—are gone.

Say goodbye.

Today, while knowledge is power*ful*, *sharing* knowledge is the real source of power. Here's why. If you look at the traditional business hierarchy—the same one adopted from the military *years* ago—the top of the pyramid represents the C-suite, the founders, or those who have the most influence by way of sheer rank or tenure. But does this make sense? I mean, executives at the top of the pyramid must (theoretically) know as much as possible about the company in order to run it effectively and to make the most informed decisions, right? But what normally happens as you traverse downwards through the ranks toward the lower levels of the pyramid?

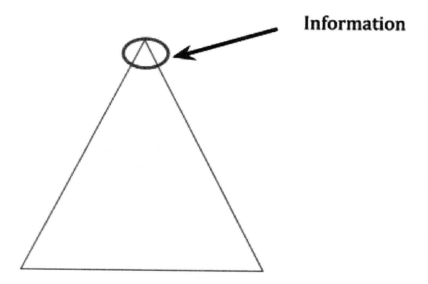

Information dissipates. Like a good old fashioned game of Telephone, knowledge gets watered down the further it permeates from the source. As a result, employees at the bottom of the totem pole often have the least business context because their focus is strictly within their own organizational silos, and without information their decision-making power—and, therefore, ability to act—is limited.

Here's what normally happens. Marketing lacks the insight that sales has from being "in the field;" sales doesn't talk with R&D and therefore can't answer customer questions about the latest and greatest because they lack the context. Accessibility to information ebbs away the further one moves from the top so much that those employees at the bottom don't have the organizational or competitive insight to make accurate and timely decisions within *their* departments. And *that* is the problem—the fact that departments, or *silos,* are structured in such a way as to restrict information exchange.

How the War on Terror Changed the Organizational Paradigm

During my tenure at Naval Special Warfare Development Group, the Joint Special Operations Command (JSOC), led by General (Ret.) Stan McChrystal, faced a completely new enemy organized in a completely new way. Gone were the days of the enemy's org chart fitting nicely into a PowerPoint slide (see Figure 1).

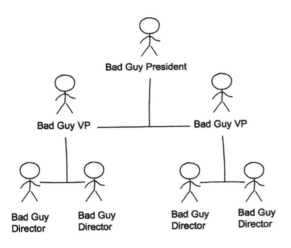

Instead, the structural makeup of this new enemy more accurately reflected that of a star cluster, or a network (see Figure 2).

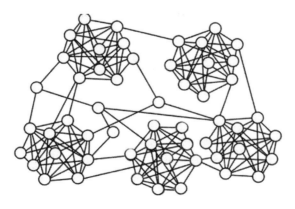

What JSOC faced was an enemy that could make decisions faster, adapt faster, and effectuate change faster than any other enemy (i.e. competitor) we had ever faced. In all honesty, we were neither prepared nor ready to face such a dynamic opponent because we were still operating within our own organizational silos instead of as one holistic unit. That is, the organizational components of JSOC such as the Army, Navy, Air Force, and others were all kicking ass on the battlefield every night and winning *their* fights, but as a whole—as one whole unit—JSOC was losing the war. We were competing against each other for air assets, mission priorities, and other operational "things" that only hindered our (read: the United States') performance.

Furthermore, we soon learned that the structure under which we worked was totally outdated. At the time, a service member "on the ground" would face a threat. He would then send a request "up" the chain of command to act on that threat, wait for a decision to be made by a leader who had "greater" strategic context, and then wait even *longer* for that decision to be sent back down. Not exactly ideal in a dynamic and constantly changing competitive landscape. And guess what? Business is no different.

What We Learned from the Enemy

The enemy's decision-making process wasn't faster than ours—they were just closer to the problem, which *enabled* them to make faster decisions. No matter how hard we worked, how fast we moved, or how straight we shot, if there were more obstacles to and more uncertainty in our decision-making process than in that of the enemy, then we were going to lose every single time. Back then, for one of our soldiers on the ground to act, we had to go through a long, drawn-out process of authorization, whereas al Qaeda only needed to make a phone call. Call me crazy, but it seems like simple physics—any object in motion will continue in motion with the same speed and in the same direction unless acted upon by an equal or greater force—and the force that stopped us was our hierarchical structure.

Additionally, any decisions the enemy made were by an individual *closest* to the problem—the person on the ground who had the greatest situational awareness, the most up-to-date information, and, consequently, the person *best positioned* to make that decision.

The Lesson Learned

Employees at the bottom must possess the same information as those at the top. Doing so allows senior leaders to focus on what they should be doing—*leading*—and keeps their focus on *the* business rather than on *your* business.

Knowledge sharing is what empowers people to make accurate and timely decisions because the information is shared across silos. When General (Ret.) Stan McChrystal was head of JSOC, he published his calendar with his information and objectives for all to see, and as a result, created a culture of transparency and inclusion amongst his people. When knowledge is openly shared, the metaphorical "left hand" knows what the "right hand" is doing, so that any stovepipes are broken down and a shared awareness with a shared purpose emerges. Immediately and over time, a culture of transparency enables employees to be proactive instead of reactive, empowered and sharing and beat their competitors because now every employee shares the same definition of *success*. Decision-making power—and, therefore, executable authority—is based on relationships, for the simple fact that the individual with the most accurate information is typically the one with the most decision-making power (i.e. influence). Such power cannot just reside at "the top" if you want to stay relevant in today's changing landscape, however. The flow of information today is too fast and too dynamic.

The New Pyramid

In order to act with the size and scope of a mega-company but with the speed and agility of a small team, you need to turn the organizational pyramid on its head.

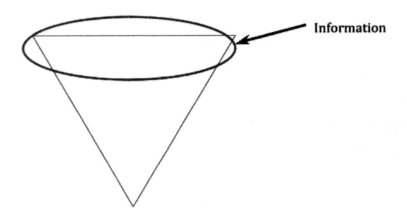

If you flip the pyramid upside down, a larger group can now share information to a wider audience, and context at the top gets pushed down to the most effective level—not the *lowest* level, but the most *effective*—such that each member is now empowered to execute in her function because she understands the direction in which the company is heading—and *why*.

What this does is allow for decisions to be made *as new information emerges* because it eliminates the travel time of knowledge transfer. Instead of a soldier having to wait for a decision to be made by a senior leader, he can now make a decision because he already understands the team's strategy, purpose, and values, as well as the boundaries within which to operate. By understanding the mission and sharing information, people can now operate autonomously without having to bog down the boss with silly requests.

Of course, having the right information *to* decide and a process to do so is critical, as a limited flow of information restricts the potential for superior performance. Figure one (below) highlights two driving forces behind decision-making: information and speed. As information becomes more readily available, the potential for quality decision-making increases because you have more information but you also have more complex data to sort through. However, once speed (i.e. the pressure of the day that gives rise to urgencies) is introduced, the time it takes to gloss over the "right" information ebbs away and you're left with the challenge that businesses face today: the need to make timely decisions with limited context in a constantly changing and complex environment.

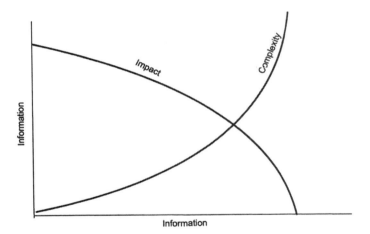

Figure 1

To avoid the pitfalls of complexity that impact decision-making in today's world requires a concerted effort to communicate up, down, and across business functions, and the main remedy to poor quality decisions in an environment where change is paramount is the *process* of generating more information to the right people.

The arrow figures below depict what happens to one's decision-making space as more relevant information comes in. The large arrow represents the direction or intent of one's business division or company—its mission or purpose. The thin arrow lines represent the amount of authority he or she has to operate in to make decisions.

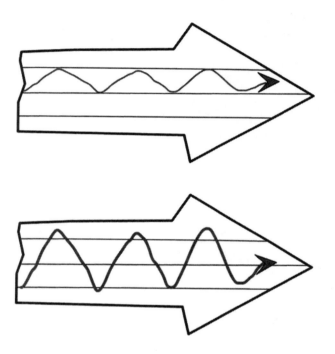

The difference between the two arrow figures above is this: the top arrow represents the individual lane or silo in which an employee operates because he or she has limited information. Once knowledge is shared, that same employee now has greater freedom of movement (i.e. decision-making power) which, in turn, frees up the senior leaders from time away from the business. As one's decision-making space increases, he or she can make a greater impact that serves the organization; she is *empowered* to act because she now has greater context on the situation. For instance, if Joe, a senior director at company X, doesn't have the context of his senior leadership team's goals and objectives, then he cannot operationalize strategy. Conversely, if the executive leadership team doesn't share their intentions or short and long term plans with direct reports, then the burden of execution is on them.

In the SEAL Teams, for instance, if we were on a mission where only half the team received the word about enemy movement to our east, then we would have lost the tactical advantage (or market share). By sharing information with the rest of the team—such as mission criteria and situation reports about the terrain and enemy (or market and competitors)—we allowed each team member the autonomy to think and act independently while aiming toward a common objective. This way, even with the increase in speed as the snowball of complexity built, numerous decisions took place while performance was maintained.

When Information Isn't Enough: Process Over Analysis

Of course, information by itself isn't everything. If your new goal is to wake up every morning and go for a run before heading into work then you could write down all the reasons for why you should—effectively analyzing the *why* behind your newfound desire. However, when 5:00 a.m. arrives, that once burning flame of motivation that shined so brightly yesterday has fizzled out. Even just motivating yourself to get out of bed, walk all the way over to your closet, change clothes, put on running shoes, and, even worse, sweating so early in the morning, has become entirely too much to think about at this moment in time. So, instead of pushing yourself through it, you roll back over and try to pick up where your dream left off.

What just happened was this: your environment wasn't set up properly to facilitate your decision. If you set up your bedroom (or wherever you sleep) for a more receptive process of decision-making, the barrier to getting out of bed withers away. For example, a more conducive environment to help facilitate your choice would be to sleep in your running clothes, place your alarm clock across the room, and have your running shoes right next to your bed so that all you have to do is wake up and swing your legs off the bedside and voilà! You're ready to go. You could even add time (i.e. speed/rate of change) to further help enable your decision and strengthen your resolve by giving yourself one minute to get out of bed.

What this hypothetical example shows is this. Having accurate information is important, but without the right process to go about operationalizing that knowledge, it's *just* information. A solid process is just as important to one's decision-making space as the information itself, and the more information employees receive—regardless of rank or tenure—the more their decision-making space widens—along with their ability to act.

This was the exact solution JSOC found that enabled it to win in a constantly changing environment. After being restructured from a hierarchy into a network, JSOC improved its ROI from executing eighteen missions per month in the early stages of the war to over three hundred per month a few years later—simply by changing the environment in which we conducted daily business. Specifically, we altered our practices to include:

- *An internal operating rhythm that created consistency— and therefore trust—between "silos."*

- *Transparent flow of information, mission priorities, and lessons learned so we could improve as an organization.*

- *Clear guidance from senior leadership on roles, responsibilities and expectations.*

Today's competitive landscape is constantly morphing, and hoarding knowledge is certainly not the key to success. If you want to stay relevant, then you, your team, and your company must be willing to constantly adapt for purpose, which only happens when you share knowledge with your people.

Putting It All Together

On April 15, 2013, 2 improvised explosive devices were set near the finish line of the Boston Marathon, killing 3 people and injuring 260 others. A four-day manhunt ensued, during which the city of Boston shut down public transit and placed inhabitants on curfews for their own safety.

Meanwhile, local, state, and federal authorities made preparations to pursue and apprehend the two suspects, ultimately identified as Tamerlan Tsarnaev and Dzhokhar Tsarnaev, while businesses, citizens, and political offices did everything they could to treat survivors and help in the investigation.

Despite the horrible tragedy and the associated chaos, a shared purpose emerged; a community centered around the theme of "Boston strong" that united people toward one goal, one objective: to apprehend the perpetrators. This shared purpose compelled people and organizations to put self-interests aside and work collaboratively toward a common front. The limited resources across local, state, and governmental agencies involved would have otherwise incited turf battles for control and involvement, but not in this case. Instead, leaders at every level chose to shoot, move, and communicate *as a team*—to perform, adapt, and lead— as a means toward achieving their shared objective.

After the bombs went off, law enforcement authorities went into a "read and react" mode of vigilance and perseverance as they received new bits of information that allowed them to anticipate next steps. Once a certain threshold of information and awareness was obtained, their purpose escalated to a new standard of performance, and it was successful because they learned how to shoot, move, and communicate (or perform, adapt, and lead) on the fly, and to do so *as a team*.

Boston's success in their rapid and efficient response to the bombings was the result of multiple factors, many of which reflect the principles that I've outlined in this book. Let's start with the 5C's of Chaos:

Competence

Emergency responders need to be ready and willing at a moment's notice. The toll such stress takes on the mind, body, and spirit can only be fathomed by those who endure the uncertainty that the inevitable call will come whenever his or her knowledge is needed. Nobody wants to answer an emergency, but when the time comes, emergency responders possess the skill and will to do so.

Character and Confidence

To serve as an emergency responder requires the same job-hiring tactic Ernest Shackleton employed before he set out on the *Endurance*: finding the right individual fit. To operate in the face of uncertainty day after day as an emergency responder requires a strong degree of mental and emotional resolve, not to mention the confidence to be ready for any situation.

Curiosity

This is perhaps the most intriguing part of the 5C model with respect to Boston's emergency responders. In the tragic wake of 9/11, emergency response units had to rethink their approach; they had to examine how they were set up for success as individual agencies and as a consortium of state and federal partners. In addition, of course, to the unspeakable suffering of that day, what the chaos of 9/11 in New York also incited was curiosity. Every person, team, agency, and organization in America wanted to know what they could do to improve their security and their contributions as Americans. As a result, this curiosity has circled back to spawn more and more competence, thus avoiding any tendency to become complacent. Boston's first responders were undoubtedly better prepared to face an act of terrorism than they would've been had 9/11 never happened, and their organized and well-orchestrated response reflected this. In many ways, America's complacency fell alongside the towers that day, but in its place, phoenix-like, was a newborn curiosity that inspired strengthened efforts across the board to prevent and address acts of terrorism. Our complacency led to chaos, which forced us to adapt, and in so doing, created a perpetual curiosity to stay competent.

The Boston Bombings are also a real-world example of the PAL Model[©] put into action. Let's look more closely at Boston's successes, as I see them, in each component of PAL:

Performance (Shoot!)

The first component—shoot—doesn't necessarily reflect the physical action of pulling a trigger, but rather aiming for the same objective and sharing the same purpose. Second, each operator moves in the same general direction—physically and mentally—as the rest of the team, and in so doing, facilitates greater *efficiency of movement* through mutually supportive roles (remember how no individual is smarter than a group?). Finally, each individual component was in direct communication with others to breed situational awareness. As a result, the overall performance of the group continually improved.

Physical

The proper physical resources, such as people, logistics, and public transportation, were coordinated such that the city of Boston was organizationally fit enough to execute across multiple districts in real time. More on this below (see Ants).

Mental

The ability to see the "big picture" across different participating partners helped put the so-called pieces of the puzzle together not only more efficiently, but effectively, too. This cross-pollination of roles and responsibilities between local, state, and federal authorities enabled better decision making and a reduction of duplicative efforts. As an example of cross-pollination, the Massachusetts National Guard was activated under Boston police's command and jurisdiction, which served two purposes. First, it created a force multiplier effect. More security personnel created a larger footprint across Boston, thus minimizing the suspects' chances of escape. Second, the support from National Guard freed up more police officers to do their jobs. While conglomeration of federal and state authorities allowed more police officers on the scene, it also served as a huge morale and confidence booster for senior leaders. With greater security personnel on the ground, public transit could stay open for the public to leave the area.

Emotional

There was more than just right and wrong involved with this case. The personal pride that Bostonians take in their city is admirable to say the least, and success in apprehending the cowardly culprits who bombed innocent people resonated at a deep level.

Spiritual

The shared purpose was what ultimately defined success in finding the perpetrators. There was no ambiguity about the fact that what the Tsarnaev brothers had done was a despicable act, and it galvanized the community in support of the law enforcement agencies who were doing what needed to be done.

Adaptability (Move!) and Leadership (Communicate!)

As mentioned earlier, adaptability ultimately relies upon one's capacity to: 1) self-renew and 2) self-organize. What was so interesting about the chaos that enveloped Boston was how the city handled it—just like ants.

What We Can Learn From Ants

I don't know about you, but I don't like bugs for the simple fact that they're annoying. Flies, ants, cockroaches, they may all have a place in this world but it certainly isn't in my living room. Of course, killing only one ant doesn't do any good; you have to eliminate the entire colony, because that's how ants survive.

In fact, that's how communities survive—and thrive—amidst chaos, and that's how Boston prevailed under a blanket of uncertainty in such a short amount of time.

Just as no single individual is smarter than a group of people, ant colonies thrive from the collective intelligence of the group. No ant colony can survive without information being passed from one to the other. They're tiny creatures, so being out in the real world poses a direct threat to their lives, which means they need to find the quickest path to a food source before they get stomped. More so, with so many ants in a colony, there must be clear roles and responsibilities for who goes where and when, and it is this systemic awareness that plays to the power of ants. The individual actions of many—most without a clear idea of the "big picture"—set the conditions for the overall success and self-preservation of the group because each ant trusts the ant in front of and behind him (or her).

Interesting, though, is the fact that there is no central authority figure, no "main" ant (besides the queen) dishing out orders or managing each other ant's role. I mean, can you imagine the challenge of allocating roles and responsibilities to *millions* of tiny little ant workers? Not this guy.

Instead, the colony as a whole relies upon the individual interactions and relationships that interconnect the whole throughout a long chain of workers for success, as each ant must be the right "fit" for the role.

Depending on environmental conditions, ant colonies determine daily how many ants they will need to send out for food. What's even more interesting is the fact that their personal sight is challenged (because it's nonexistent) which means that they can only share information through touch and smell. To identify one ant from another, for example, they use their antennae to smell for similar scents. If the scent is different, then that ant hails from a different nest.

Prior to leaving their beloved nest every day, those ants who go out in search of food—let's just call them (creatively) searchers—wait for the ant scouts (those working outside the nest) to return back to the nest after patrolling for food, and as they do, both the searchers and the scouts "high five" each other's antennae for two reasons. First, it's to ensure that it's the right ant. By identifying the scent of the scout ants, the searchers can follow the trail from where they came. Second, the rate at which searcher ants encounter scouts tells them when it's safe to leave the nest. If the time between interactions is too long, then there might be some big bad humans out there, too much sun, or some other unknown that obstructs progress. In a nutshell, it works like this: the more frequent the "high fives," the safer it is because everybody's back. The less frequent, then it's to better hold off since more of the ant's buddies are still searching. Once the searching begins, more ants join the (search) party.

What's so fascinating about ants is that no *direct leadership* is required. Rather, results are produced as a byproduct of the *adaptive leadership* wielded through interconnectivity—relationships—that enables them to continually *adapt* based on the information and interactions they encounter. Searcher ants will stay out until they find food. The more food there is, the faster they return; the less food, the longer they stay out. No single ant decides if "today" is a good day to look for food. Rather, each ant reads and reacts off the others and fills the gap based on their rate of communication. It's amazing how such simple, consistent interactions can drive such complex behavior.

What does this have to do with Boston? Plenty. For the law enforcement agencies to have won in this constantly changing environment—where information was coming in faster than you can say this sentence—they needed three things:

Trust

There was complete trust in every agency's skill and will—competence and character—to perform.

Communication

Information flow was paramount so as to defer authority to the person(s) closest to the problem. What this did was enable the law enforcement movement *as a whole* to move and adapt *together* rather than just individual pieces. In other words, everyone had to be able to execute and make decisions without waiting for approval; they needed greater decision-making space that afforded them greater freedom of movement—and therefore influence.

A "We" Mindset

There was only a single purpose that local, state and federal authorities shared after the bombings went off: to catch the perpetrators. There was no delineation of authority, no hierarchy through which to request approvals, and no central figurehead dishing out orders to each agency to do *this* or do *that*. Instead, everybody knew what to do because they shared their status with others, which allowed them to adapt to the situation as it unfolded.

Curiosity (again!)

There's one last piece of the puzzle: the learning piece. As you will recall from the cycling of the 5Cs, curiosity is the foundation upon which future increased competence is built. Just as security improvements were made post-9/11, post-Boston Bombing, first responders naturally cycled back into a space of vigilance—curiosity—to keep their competencies up to par with current day threats.

Even in the wake of these successes, first responders at both Boston's local level and the nation's federal level recognized that there is always something to be learned from chaos. Remember the AAR? Just eleven months after the bombings took place, the Majority Staff of the House Committee on Homeland Security had created recommendations for strengthening the relationship between federal and local law enforcement in future cases such as Boston's. In other words, even though the situation had reached as satisfactory a resolution as possible (one bomber dead, the other incarcerated), officials understood that there was plenty more to learn, and redoubled their efforts toward creating an even stronger response in the unfortunate event of a "next time."

♦♦♦

Like the ant colony, people and organizations make decisions and take action based on the current realities they face, which is fueled by information. Their behaviors are shaped by what they anticipate will happen next. A complete understanding of the environment is what allows this accurate anticipation, and it only comes from the diversity and fusion of information that, together, paints a clear picture of what to expect.

Every mission we ever planned was different from the previous one. Each one had its own unique identifiers, pieces of intelligence that necessitated a different tactic, and alternative courses of action. Furthermore, each bit of information came from a hodgepodge of governmental agencies, so fusing the intelligence together was critical in order to assemble a complete picture.

Summary

Trying to control chaos is an exercise in futility, but coordinating the elements that comprise it is not. The innovative advantage for any organization is not equipment, technology, or people, but rather the ability to fuse *all* of these elements together into one cohesive unit that serves the organization holistically *as a team,* and adapts as necessary to stay relevant. This is the function of leadership—overseeing the performance aspects of yourself or of the company, and finding opportunities to adapt and stay relevant.

Information flow, decision-making, people, and resources all operate more efficiently when the right systems and processes are in place to optimize all of the factors that create high-performance. One last example. Former mayor Michael Bloomberg's office was sheer pandemonium—*by design.* The completely open floor plan forced and fostered a culture of inclusivity and personal interaction that created more information sharing. In theory, the office plan might've appeared chaotic, but in practice, with "its wheels set in motion," it became a living, breathing organism that shifted as necessary because the proverbial left hand knew what the right hand was doing (an observation that I do *not* intend as a political pun). Since everybody operated under the same roof, in the same space, and at the same time, there was no hiding because people and purposes were fused together such that there was no hiding behind other "initiatives" or personal agendas. Instead, everybody was in the center of the action all the time because *they created* the action. They were both leaders *and* followers.

Key Takeaways

- *Boston successfully handling of the marathon bombings was a reflection of both the 5Cs and PAL Model© put into action.*

- *Ants are naturals when it comes to performance and adaptability. Just like a colony of ants, an organization's ability to perform consistently over time stems from their ability to adapt.*

- *Adaptability depends on trust, communication, and a "we" mindset that instills a shared purpose.*

Final Chapter

E verybody has the opportunity to quit BUD/S, a chance to leave their job or team by their own free will, but to abandon that which defines you for the sake of a more benign career never made sense to me. All the reason and rationale were there for me to leave—especially after all my ridiculously close calls—and nobody would have frowned upon it. But doing so would have lacked two major components: the purpose and passion to change.

I was happy where I was, and I had become stronger because of these unique experiences. I viewed the crazy events in my life as opportunities to demonstrate personal resolve, resiliency, and leadership. They each made me stronger both as a SEAL and as a person.

The value of having the aforementioned ingredients of success in your back pocket is that they help you know when to assess, when to adapt, and when to just *do*. They are fundamental practices that enable organizational fitness, thereby allowing you to sustain superior performance. Not only is the ability to shoot, move, and communicate better or faster than the enemy important, but it's also the discipline to reflect and learn through increased performance capacities, the skill and will to adapt, and the courage to lead that enable you to become better *as an individual and as a team*. When these ingredients are shared throughout a company, they create an unmatched capability with which nobody else can compete; one that defines the organization as *fitter* than all the rest. More so, it creates a *community* to which people feel they belong. Knowledge sharing is what drives results, but it's personal leadership that seizes the opportunity out of a devotion to oneself, others, and the mission that sustains superior performance.

◆◆◆

I don't believe in any specific model for change. There is no "right" way to go about change, because the unexpected is just that—unexpected, and therefore unplanned. How do you plan for the unknown? You don't, but you can definitely have the confidence to *try*; to make decisions that you *believe* will lead you down the right road, and the self-efficacy to make it happen. When you're receiving incoming fire by the enemy, it doesn't matter in which direction you move just as long as you *move*. Providing direction is a staple of leadership—to find certainty in uncertain situations. *Any* decision is better than *no* decision, but *no* decision is still *a* decision. Of course, if there is a framework you like, then then by all means use it. But use it as a guide rather than a rule. Be willing to pick and choose the good, and discard the bad if certain aspects are simply unfit for the situation. Things always change.

◆◆◆

There's one final thing; one last piece to the puzzle, and it's something that no one else can give or teach you. Between the PAL Model© and the 5Cs, you now understand the tools that enable top-tier performance. What cannot be taught, or conveyed in any book, though, is how to find that last piece, the tiny but critical spark that ignites your inspiration, your passion, and leads you down a road of purpose and meaning. I found it in the SEAL Teams; as a college kid, training in the gym and dreaming of BUD/S; as a

SEAL Trainee living through hell week(s); and as a Team Guy, living and fighting alongside my brothers, and staying long after my nine lives were up. The dream of whom and what I wanted to be was enough to carry me through, but that was just me. Whatever it is that drives *you* to get out of bed an extra hour early in the morning, to make the sacrifices necessary to give 100 percent of yourself day after day—this is the thing that only *you* can find. And once you find it, there's no turning back. It's ineffable, but it's essential. It's the key that sets all of the other parts in motion and is typically discovered unintentionally amidst the unexpected. When the unknown presents itself, don't fear it. Embrace it. For there's always opportunity in chaos.

Bibliography

Intro to Performance

Wong., L. *Developing Adaptive Leaders: The Crucible Experience of Operation Iraqi freedom.* 2004. Retrieved from http://www.carlisle.army.mil/ssi .

Pressfield, Steven. *The War Of Art: Winning the Inner Creative Battle.* FastPencil Premiere, 2010. Kindle Edition. 37.

Filling the Knowledge Gap

Collins, Jim, and Morton Hansen. *Great By Choice.* New York: HarperCollins, 2011.

Industry Analysis Case Study B: Southwest Airlines Strategy. Captain Marvel. PDF. https://assurantcorp.com/inc/eexcel/resources/e.excel_ia_case2_wb.pdf.

Schlesinger, Jennifer. "Ten Minutes That Saved Southwest Airlines' Future." CNBC. July 15, 2011. http://www.cnbc.com/id/43768488#.

Govindarajan, Vijay, and Julie B. Lang. "Southwest Airlines Corporation." Tuck School of Business at Dartmouth. July 9, 2002. PDF. http://mba.tuck.dartmouth.edu/pdf/2002-2-0012.pdf.

Just When You Thought You Had Enough

"Chinese heaven and hell." Wisdom Commons. http://www.wisdomcommons.org/wisbits/3241-in-heaven-we-feed-each-other

Heifetz, Ronald A., Marty Linsky, and Alexander Grashow. "The Practice of Adaptive Leadership: Tools and Tactics for Changing Your Organization and the World." Harvard Business Review Press, 2009. Kindle Edition. 14.

Owens, B., and D. Hekman. "Modeling How to Grow: An Inductive Examination of Humble Leader Behaviors, Contingencies, and Outcomes." *Academy of Management Journal,* 2012. Vol. 55, No. 4, 787–818. http://dx.doi.org/10.5465/amj.2010.0441.

Intro to Leadership

Heifetz, Ronald A., Marty Linsky, and Alexander Grashow. "The Practice of Adaptive Leadership: Tools and Tactics for Changing Your Organization and the World." Harvard Business Review Press, 2009. Kindle Edition. 14.

Pressfield, Steven. *The War Of Art: Winning the Inner Creative Battle.* FastPencil Premiere, 2010. Kindle Edition. 18.

Csikszentmihalyi, M. *Flow: The Psychology of Optimal Performance.* New York: Harper Perennial, 1990.

Parnell, David. "Counterinsurgency Expert John Nagl, ON The Parallels of Business and War." Forbes. December 8, 2014. http://www.forbes.com/sites/davidparnell/2014/12/08/counterinsurgency-john-nagl-business-and-war/2/.

Catmull, Ed, and Amy Wallace. *Creativity, Inc.: Overcoming the Unseen Forces That Stand in the Way of True Inspiration.* New York: Random House, 2014. Kindle Edition. Kindle Locations 773-774.

Schneider, D., and C. Goldwasser. "Be a Model Leader of Change." *Management Review,* 1998. Vol. 87, No. 3, 41. Retrieved from Business Source Premier database.

Jacobs, T. O., and M. G. Sanders (n.d.). "Principles for building the profession: SOF experience." Email correspondence.

Olney, Buster. "Fast Feet, But Faulk Is an Even Quicker Thinker." *New York Times.* February 1, 2002. http://www.nytimes.com/2002/02/01/sports/football/01RAMS.html.

Wheatley, Margaret J. *Leadership and the New Science: Discovering Order in a Chaotic World.* Berrett-Koehler Publishers, 2006. Kindle Edition. Kindle Locations 2228-2229.

"Our View: Adaptability crucial for military in today's world." Fay Observer. February 27, 2015. http://www.fayobserver.com/opinion/editorials/our-view-adaptability-crucial-for-military-in-today-s-world/article_695bb97f-31f2-547d-a154-4688a4ebc4fe.html

About The Author

J eff is an executive coach and consultant who helps individuals, teams, and organizations enhance their performance, adaptability, and leadership capacities to align with organizational objectives.

Visit him online at www.tieroneleadership.com

You can also measure your adaptability by visiting his personal website www.adaptabilitycoach.com.